Decorating for CHRISTMAS

Five Festive Themes with 70 Craft Projects for Your Home

CAROLYN SCHULZ

Reader's Digest

THE READER'S DIGEST ASSOCIATION, INC.
Pleasantville, New York/Montreal

Dedication

I dedicate this book to my devoted father Bernard, who taught me how to observe, to my generous mother Wanda, who taught me the love of creating with my hands, and to my patient husband Tony, who has lived with Christmas every day for the past four years. Their constant love and support have made all this possible.

A Reader's Digest Book
Edited and produced by David & Charles Publishers

Project Editor: Heather Dewhurst
Photography by Caroline Arber
Styling by Tina Guillory
Illustrations by Chris King
Book design by Anita Ruddell

First published in Great Britain in 1996

Library of Congress Cataloging-in-Publication Data

Schulz, Carolyn.
Decorating for Christmas : five festive themes with 70 craft projects for your home / Carolyn Schulz.
p. cm.
Includes index.
ISBN 0-89577-885-8
1. Christmas decorations. 2. Handicraft. I. Title
TT900.C4S34 1996
745.594'12–dc20 96-14090

Printed in Great Britain

Contents

Introduction

WITH THE INCREASING AMOUNT of leisure time available to us today, more and more people are becoming involved in home-decorating. In addition to pursuing sports and other traditional hobbies, we are spending more time improving our domestic environment. We want to make our homes more attractive, and more comfortable.

Within the sphere of home decor, it has become more and more fashionable to use a theme incorporating color and design. With its appeal to the eye, it becomes quite natural to extend this idea of coordinating design into the special decoration of our homes that takes place once a year at Christmas.

In this book I have singled out five distinctive decorating themes for the festive season, in addition to alternative color themes — tartan, toyland, Scandinavian, Victorian, and country — and have given a host of ideas for decorating your tree, table, and home within each particular theme. For example, the tartan theme explores the use of perfectly ruched bows in its decorations, while the toyland theme will delight all children with its candy garland, Santa stocking (opposite), and teddy bear tree ornaments. The Scandinavian theme focuses on traditional Norwegian and Danish festive decorations, such as woven hearts and sheaves of wheat, while the Victorian theme shows what you can make with a profusion of lace, ribbons, and pearls. Finally, the country theme takes its inspiration from nature and shows how to make decorations for the tree, room, and table from natural materials.

When you decide you want to choose a theme, you don't need to have a clean or blank canvas on which to start working. From Christmases past, there are sure to be tiny treasures, perhaps lovingly made by grandparents or fashioned by tiny hands over the generations. Look at what ornaments you have and put those that have special meaning to one side. Look carefully at the special ornaments you have kept. What is it that makes them special? Do some of them represent special events, occasions, or people in your life or the lives of your family? You can hang these ornaments at strategic positions all over your tree, no matter what theme you follow. Let them personalize your tree and remind you of the special thoughts that go with them.

Despite the increased commercialism of the Christmas season, it is still a very special time of year. It has a different meaning to each of us, and we can express this through the decorations we use throughout the home. Themes can be more than coordinating colors, textures, and shapes. They can express peace and joy, or fun and laughter, and I believe that, through a theme, you can share with others a little of yourself and your personality. I hope this book will give you the confidence to experiment with making and using themed Christmas decorations, and help you to create a unique and special look in your home.

CHAPTER 1

Decorating the Christmas Tree:

A Step-by-Step Guide

DECORATING THE CHRISTMAS TREE can be one of the most pleasurable experiences of the holiday preparations, providing the creator with a true sense of achievement. Often we are harassed with too much to do and too little time in which to do it. With the suggestions in this step-by-step guide, I hope to provide you with the means of creating your perfect Christmas tree, in addition to making it an enjoyable and enduring tradition.

Mental attitude is very important. Don't feel that you have to decorate the entire tree in one session. There is nothing worse than having the whole family standing around, with their favorite ornaments in hand, impatiently waiting for you to hang the lights or the garland. In this situation, everyone ends up frustrated, and reality often fails to resemble the creation envisaged.

I prefer to trim the tree by working through the basic preliminary stages over a few days, usually after the children have gone to bed. Each morning they eagerly look to see how the design is developing. They know that I am performing the tedious tasks that are the background for the fun to come. Usually we have a tree-trimming party the weekend before Christmas, and the whole family joins in to put their ornaments into position.

I start by positioning the tree in its stand or container for a couple of days to give the branches a chance to settle. If you are using an artificial tree, you will need to spread out the branches. A little steam can help the artificial silk trees look fresh and lively.

If electric lights are used, these must be placed in position before progressing to any other stages. This is one of the most important basics, and the one I like the least. For this reason, I have tried scrimping on the number of lights and even bribed other members of the family to put them up. The fact is, nothing can enhance the design of your tree more than properly placed lights, so take your time, and grin and bear it!

Draping a garland and attaching the bows follows the placement of lights. At the completion of each stage, your tree will be dressed. If you prefer, or if there is not enough time available to continue, this will provide you with a decorated tree, effective in the simplicity of its design.

STEP 1

LIGHTS

There are many types of lights available today. There are colored lights and lights that flash; there are musical lights and lights in various shapes, such as candles and figures. My favorites are small crystal lights, which are used only as a source of lighting up and emphasizing the ornaments on the tree.

Lighting is very important on a Christmas tree. The more light there is available, the more effective your tree will look. Miniature lights placed on the tree will brighten up the space where they are placed, adding depth as well as sparkle. Spotlights emphasize the shape of the tree and provide a surface glow to the other tree decorations.

I like to use lots of lights and collect inexpensive strands of small plain crystal lights. I start at the top of the tree and work down, with the lights plugged in so I can see where they are being placed. With more than one string of lights, I find it easier to work down one section of the tree for each strand. Choose lights with green wire for green trees; attach the wire to the tree branches with 4-inch pieces of green florist's wire to hide the wire as much as possible. Work along a branch from the trunk out to the tip, and back again.

STEP 2

GARLANDS

The garland trim ties together the various sections of the decorated tree. There are many things that can be used as a tree garland; a few ideas are illustrated on page 11, but why not use your imagination to create an original garland for your chosen theme?

Garlands can be draped on the tree in several different ways. The more traditional way, as seen on the Victorian tree, is the swag pattern, which is more formal. There are several variations to the swag, which can include hanging two or three strands at a time, or crisscrossing the swags over each other from both directions. On the Scandinavian tree I have strung the flag garlands in vertical lines down the tree. An alternative you could consider is running twisted ribbon from the top of the tree to the base.

Whichever garland or method of draping the Christmas tree you choose, it is best to start at the back of the top of the tree and work down the branches. Use green florist's wire to attach the garland to the branches. Step back from the tree frequently while you are working to survey the effect of the garland. Then, if necessary, any alterations can be made before progressing too far.

STEP 3
BOWS

Decorative ribbon bows can add the finishing touch to your Christmas tree, just as they do to gift-wrapped presents. I like to use bows to accentuate the swag design of the tree garland, making it appear as if the bows are holding the swag to the branches. Today we are quite spoiled for choice with so many different ribbons easily available, which create lovely full bows that hold their shape easily. Another of my personal favorites is wire-edged ribbon, which can be shaped to perfection (see the samples on page 11).

STEP 4
ORNAMENTS

It is at this stage of tree decoration that the true character of the tree takes shape. Within the framework of your theme, the repetition of certain ornaments will help the theme become evident.

Hang one type of ornament at a time, such as variously sized miniature packages, scattering them around the branches. Repeat with other decorations, one type at a time. Hang larger ornaments toward the bottom of the tree, and graduate the sizes up toward the top, where you can place smaller ones.

Making Bows

Many people shy away from making their own bows, thinking that they are too difficult, or perhaps they have tried unsuccessfully. I have chosen three of the easiest bows, using techniques I find foolproof. Try them—you will be pleasantly surprised!

Single Bow

Cut two strips of the chosen material (ribbon, lace, fabric, etc.) measuring 13 inches and 18 inches long respectively, and 1½ inches wide. Fold the shorter strip in half to find the center. Scrunch the strip along this central line, and hold it with one hand while forming loops with each of the cut ends of the paper strips with the other hand. Overlap the loops by ½-1 inch. Wrap a piece of wire around the scrunched center to secure.

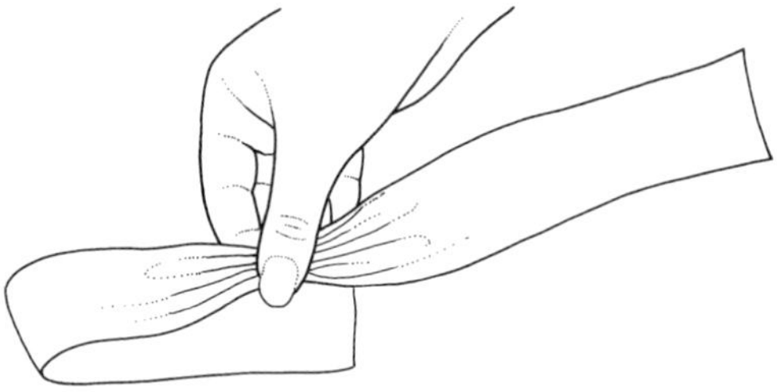

Take the longer strip and place the center over the middle of the front of the bow loops already formed. Wrap this strip around to the back of the bow, and tie the ends together in a knot, pulling tightly to hold. This forms the bow tails. Cut a V-shaped notch in the tails.

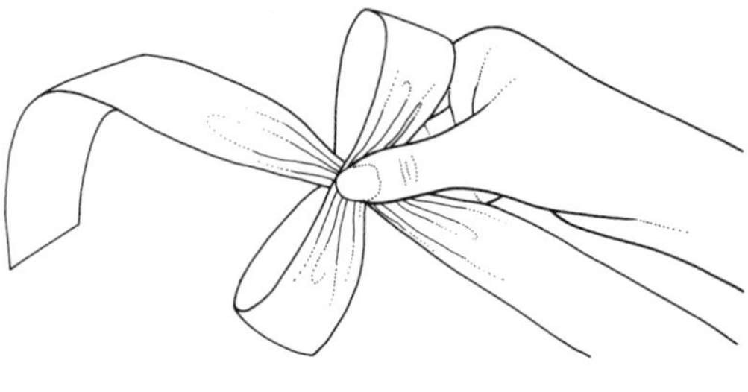

Double Bow

Cut two strips of material, as for the single bow, then cut a third strip 11 inches long. Make separate bow loops using the 13-inch and the 11-inch strips, as for the single bow. Place the small set of loops over the larger set of loops, holding them together in the center. Tie the longest strip of material around both sets of loops and knot at the back to make the bow tails for the double bow. Cut a V-shaped notch in the tails.

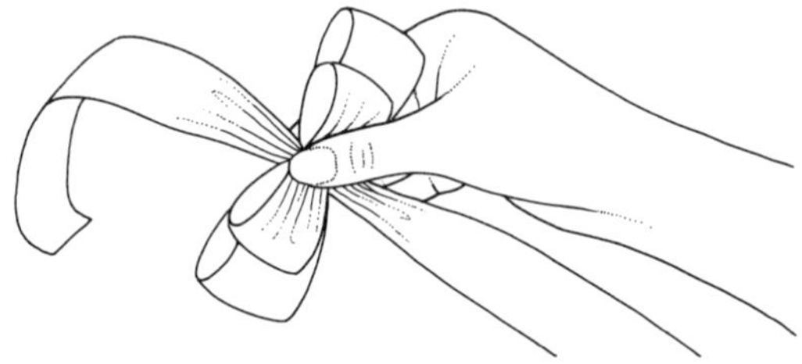

Fluffy Double-loop Bow

Make two sets of loops, as for the double bow. Wire each set together side by side. Stack the small loops over the large loops, and tie them together with an 18-inch strip of ribbon. Fluff out, and cut a V-shaped notch in the tails.

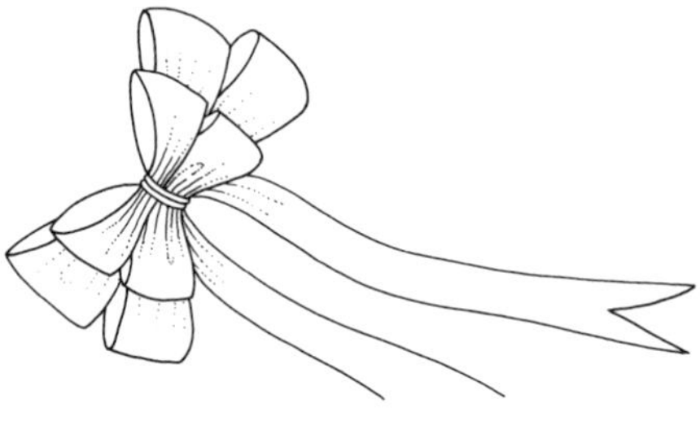

Single bows (top), double bows (center), fluffy double-loop bows (below), and a selection of tree garlands

CHAPTER 2

Color Themes

As IN HOME DECORATION, color is the most popular theme used in Christmas tree design. A color theme can mean one, two, three, or a multitude of colors. The traditional Christmas colors of bright red and green can be mixed with each other, or individually with other colors, to create many different color themes with varying effects. Often gold or silver are combined with other colors, creating an even wider selection of color themes.

Color does not need to be the exclusive element of any Christmas decorating theme. As you will see in the chapters that follow, color can very much complement another theme. Color can also make a difference in how a theme is perceived. For example, it would be very hard to produce a warm, natural country Christmas theme using varying blues and silvers. However, with the use of rustic reds and natural wheaten hues, you can obtain the warm cozy setting that cool blues and glitzy silvers never could.

When choosing a successful color theme for home decoration at Christmas, it is wise to take into consideration the existing color scheme and room decor. This does not mean that the tree and room decorations should be exactly the same as those used in the room decor. It does mean, however, that it can be important to find color combinations that will blend in with the colors and setting that already exist. The final result should complement the total look.

In this chapter I have chosen two color combinations, and I have duplicated the tree and home decorations in each of these combinations. Each of the two themes has gold as the prominent color, which is then combined with a secondary color to produce dramatically different results. Notice the difference that the choice of a second color makes.

The white and gold combination of colors lends itself very well to many room settings and color schemes, creating a subtle elegance. The combination of silver and white creates a similar effect. Although not necessary, you could add a third color, possibly a color chosen from the room decor (such as burgundy, pink, navy, or peach, etc.), to accent the color scheme of the room. By introducing a third color, you can very easily create a new theme with a different effect, which could make it blend even more closely with the room setting.

Because red is considered a Christmas color, one can get away with introducing it into most room settings. However, the red and gold color combination is not as versatile when it comes to introducing other accent colors. Being an aggressive color, red can have an overpowering effect in a room setting. However, by carefully manipulating the amount of red decoration that is mixed in with the gold, you can control whether your Christmas tree reflects a rich, festive warmth or an overly strong boldness.

White and Gold Tree

For my first theme, I have chosen to combine gold with a pearl white for subtle elegance. The pearl softens the glitter of the gold to make it more subdued.

Miniature crystal lights reflect on the sequined ornaments to produce a soft glow on this exquisite color combination. Fluffy double bows formed out of paper ribbon hold up double swags of thick gold cord. The tree branches are loaded with glistening ornaments, from miniature Christmas favors, gemstone baubles, and fashionable angels, to small gift packages. Crowning it all is a glorious pearl-studded star.

Pincraft ornaments (page 16)

Red and Gold Tree

For this color theme, I have combined red with gold to achieve bold, brilliant color. This tree is identical to my white and gold tree, except for the exchange of red for white. Sequined ornaments glisten in reflected light from the miniature crystal lights. The multifaceted gemstones reflect the red and gold colors from the ornaments, making the tree shimmer. Rich red and gold cloth balls hang beside elegant accordian angels nestling in the greenery. The branches of the tree are laden with small gift boxes and miniature Christmas favors that are decorated with a profusion of curls. The treetop star is the perfect way to finish this enticing vision of Christmas warmth and cheer.

WHITE AND GOLD TREE

RED AND GOLD TREE

Tree Decorations

The trees in this chapter are decorated with sparkling pincraft ornaments, all of which are very easy to make. In addition, accordian angels sit among fluffy double-loop bows made from gold paper ribbon. Cloth balls, Christmas favors, and gemstone ornaments complete the colorful theme.

PINCRAFT ORNAMENTS

General Instructions

These general instructions will be particularly useful to first-time pincrafters. By using these basic techniques, you can design original creations using a range of materials and color combinations.

1 Divide each plastic-foam shape into four equal sections using a pencil. Sections should run up and down the length of the shape.

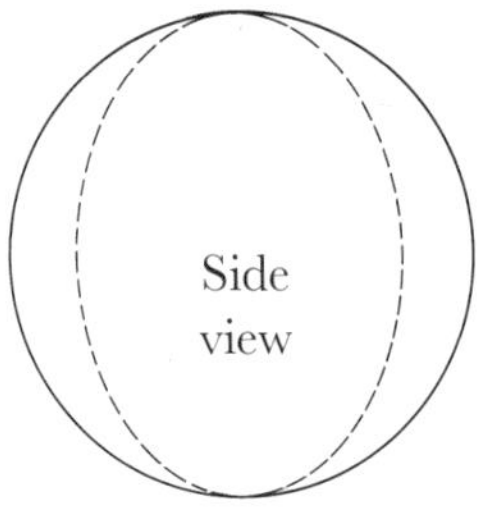

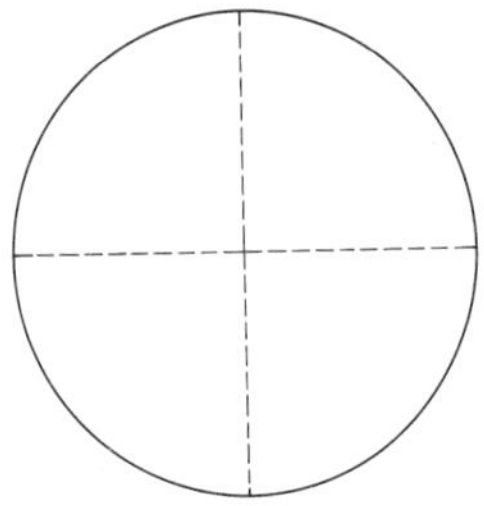

View from above

2 Cover the pencil lines with ribbon, lace, or braid, depending on the chosen design. Start by attaching one cut end of the ribbon to the top of the shape with a short pin. Run the ribbon down the side of the shape, around the bottom, and back up to the top (dividing the shape in half). Overlap the ribbon slightly and secure it with a short pin. Cut the ribbon and repeat, at right angles, over the remaining pencil line, to make four equal sections. Measure the blank spaces between the ribbon to make sure they are equal. The ribbon should be wound tightly so it does not slip off.

3 Fill in the blank spaces between the ribbon with pearls, sequins, or beads on short pins, as directed for a particular design. There are different ways in which sequin units will be used and described. Listed below are terms you may come across. Note that, unless otherwise stated, sequins are all ¼ inch cup:

Bead and sequin unit — "cup up": This means you thread a bead (if required), then a concave cup sequin, onto a short pin.

Bead and sequin unit — "cup down": This means you thread a bead (if required), then a convex cup sequin, onto a short pin.

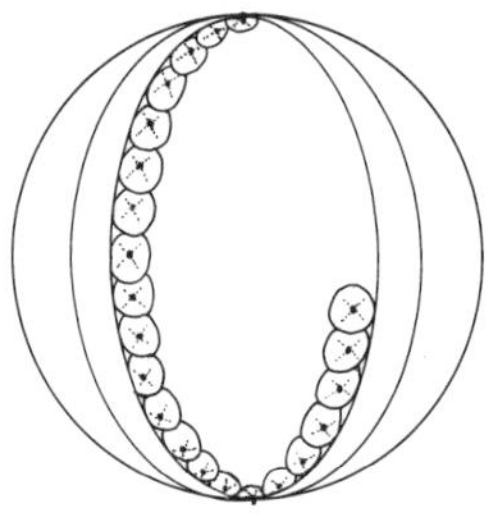

Starting at the bottom of one section, run a row of the sequin units up the edge of the ribbon to the top. Run another row of units up

Red and gold treetop star

the edge of the ribbon on the other side. Fill in the space between with rows of units.

4 To make ribbon loops at the top of the ornament, place two long pins so they are firmly secured, yet protruding, one-third of the way down from the top of the shape in the center of two opposite sections. These are guide pins and should be removed after the

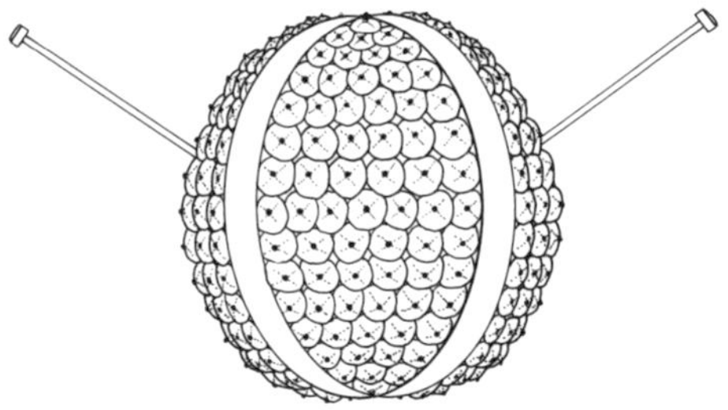

ribbon loops are completed. Attach one cut end of the ribbon to the center top of the shape. Keep the ribbon flat (do not twist it). Wind it clockwise around one guide pin and back to the center. Continue winding, this time counterclockwise, around the other pin. Check to see that this figure-of-eight set of loops is of equal length and fullness on both sides. Use short pins to secure in place.

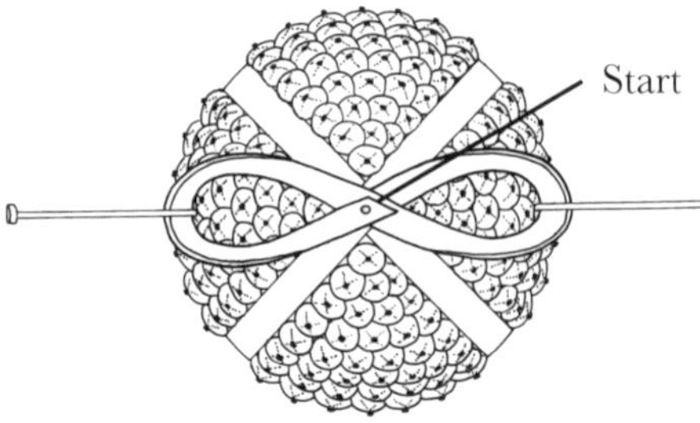

5 Make another set of loops, directly over the previous set, without cutting the ribbon. Replace the guide pins ¼ inch closer to the top of the shape. Form a second set of loops over the first ones, except a little shorter.

6 Form a set of loops at right angles over the remaining two sections of the shape, this time cutting the ribbon. Start with step 4, forming loops around guide pins placed in the other two sections.

7 Make a hanging loop by forming a large loop with 6–8 inches of ribbon. Overlap the two cut ends and attach them to the center top of the ornament using short pins.

8 Decorate the ornament, as desired.

TREETOP STAR

Materials

The materials given are for a white and gold star. The colors for the red and gold star are given in brackets.

Molded plastic-foam star, 8 inches in diameter
Gold (red) acrylic paint
Paintbrush
52 inches gold braid
Scissors
1,350 brass pins, 4 x .55mm
1,250 white (gold) pearl beads, ⅛ inch
36 white (gold or red) pearlized teardrop hat pins or corsage pins, 2 inches long
6 gold filigree cones, 1½ inches long
Glue
Florist's wire

1 Paint the star with three coats of acrylic paint on the front and back.

2 Starting at the center of one side of the star, wrap gold braid around the star, over two opposite points and back to the center. Cut the braid and repeat over the other two sets of points. Pin the cut ends to the star. Pin the braid here and there with small pins, each threaded through a pearl bead.

3 Thread a hat pin through the filigree cone. Dip the part of the pin showing below the cone in glue; place it on one of the star points. Repeat with the other five points.

4 Push a hat pin through the plastic-foam on each side of the filigree cone. Angle them so they do not poke through the other side.

5 Push a hat pin in each space at the center of the star where the braid strips cross over (six in all). Repeat on the other side.

6 Thread the small pearls onto a small pin. Poke these into the star in a line all around

White and gold treetop star

the outside edge, between the filigree cones. Place a second row just inside the first row on each side. Place two rows of pearls from the center of the star, halfway between the braid strips in the six sections of the star, to the outside edge, which is decorated with two rows of pearls. Repeat on the back. The star will now have six diamond-shaped sections outlined with two rows of pearl beads, with gold cord running through the center of the diamond shape and a filigree cone on the outside strip.

7 Randomly place small pearls threaded onto a short pin in the gold sections on each side of the gold braid. Repeat on the back.

8 Poke a hole on each side of the center of the star at the back. Glue a 4-inch length of wire in each side. Use this for attaching the star to the top of the tree.

SEQUINED MINI-BELL

MATERIALS

Plastic-foam mini-bell shape
Pencil
20 inches red or white ribbon with gold metallic diamonds, $^3/_8$ inch wide
200 brass pins, 14 x .55mm
200 gold or red cup sequins, $^1/_4$ inch
150 tiny crystal glass beads
$1^2/_3$ yards gold metallic ribbon, $^1/_4$ inch wide
2 white or gold teardrop hat pins or corsage pins, 2 inches long
2 medium crystal or gold plastic beads
1 small flat filigree gold cap

1 Divide each plastic-foam shape into four equal sections using a pencil. Sections should run up and down the length of the shape.

2 Cover the pencil lines using the ribbon with the metallic diamond design. Instead of starting at the top of the mini-bell, start by placing the first cut end of the ribbon into the hole at the bottom or wide end, run the ribbon around the shape and back to the hole, pushing the second cut end into the hole, too. Use short pins to hold the ribbon in place on the edge of the hole. Repeat with a second piece of ribbon at right angles to the first.

3 Fill in the sections between the ribbon with "cup up" bead and sequin units, using gold or red sequins and tiny clear beads. Work in rows from the outside toward the center.

4 Make a double set of ribbon loops over two opposite sequined sections, using gold metallic ribbon.

Sequined mini-bells

5 Make a hanging loop with gold metallic ribbon. Position it to run right and left over the ribbon loops, placed so when the ornament is held up by the hanger, the ribbon loops are on each side of the mini-bell.

6 To decorate and complete the ornament, make two of the following units and place one each into the center top (over the ribbon loops) and center bottom (over hole) of the mini-bell. Onto a teardrop hat pin (white for the white/gold bell; red for the red/gold bell), thread on one medium plastic bead (crystal for white/gold; gold for red/gold) and a flat filigree cap (convex).

SEQUINED FILIGREE OVAL

Materials

2 inch oval (or spherical) molded plastic-foam shape
40 inches gold metallic grosgrain ribbon, 1/8 inch wide
400 brass pins, 14 x .55mm
350 tiny clear or red glass beads
350 mother-of-pearl or red cup sequins, 1/4 inch
40 inches gold metallic grosgrain ribbon, 3/8 inch wide
1 gold filigree cone
2 white or gold teardrop hat pins, 2 inches long
12 long dressmaker's pins
6 small amber or red cut-glass beads
6 medium white pearl or gold oat beads
6 small white pearl or gold oat beads
6 white or gold pearl beads, 1/8 inch
1 gold rhinestone bead
1 plastic gold cap

1 Divide each plastic-foam shape into six equal sections using a pencil. Make sure that the sections run along the length of the shape (up and down).

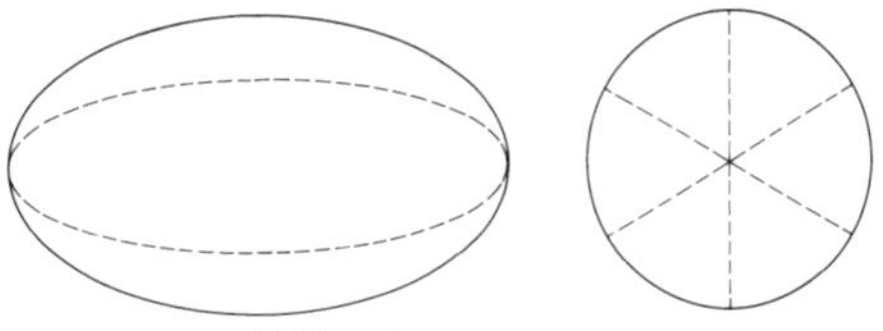

2 Cover the pencil lines with the narrower gold ribbon, and secure with brass pins.

3 Fill in the blank sections with "cup up" bead and sequin units, using clear beads and mother-of-pearl sequins for the white/gold ornament, or red beads and red sequins for the red/gold ornament.

4 Place one set of double loops across two opposite sequined sections with wider ribbon.

5 Make a hanging loop using narrower ribbon. Position the loop to run right and left over the ribbon loops, placed so when the ornament is held up by the hanging loop, the ribbon loops are on each side of the oval shape.

6 Bend the six prongs of the filigree cone so they hug the oval shape when placed at the bottom of the ornament. Pass a hat pin through from the tip to attach the cone to the bottom of the decoration. Position the prongs to extend into the sequined sections, removing any sequin units if necessary.

7 Make up six units of a long pin passed through a cut-glass bead and a medium pearl oat bead (white pearl for the white/gold ornament; gold for the red/gold ornament). Place one of these units at the point between each of the prongs of the filigree cone.

8 Make up six units of a long pin passed through a small pearl oat bead (white pearl for white/gold; gold for the red/gold ornament). Place one of these units in front of each of the large oat units.

Sequined filigree ornaments and round sequin decorations

9 Make up six units of a long pin passed through a small pearl bead (white pearl for white/gold; gold for the red/gold). Place two of these in the three prongs with cut-outs.

10 To complete the sequined filigree ornament, place one final unit of a hat pin (white for the white/gold; gold for the red/gold), passed through a gold rhinestone bead and a gold plastic cap (convex), in the center of the top of the decoration, over the top of the ribbon loops.

ROUND SEQUIN DECORATION

MATERIALS

Round (or oval) molded plastic-foam shape, 2 inches in diameter
Pencil
20 inches gold-edged (white or red) satin ribbon, 3/8 inch wide
20 inches gold-edged (white or red) satin ribbon, 1/8 inch wide
1 2/3–2 1/4 yards gold metallic ribbon, 1/4 inch wide
200 white or gold pearls, 1/8 inch
500 brass pins, 14 x .55mm
125 mother-of-pearl or red cup sequins, 1/4 inch
125 tiny clear or red glass beads
150 matte gold cup sequins, 1/4 inch
2 white or gold teardrop hat pins, 2 inches long
3 tiny gold beads
1 small crystal or red cut-glass bead
2 gold filigree caps
1 medium crystal or red cut-glass bead
1 large crystal or red cut-glass bead

1 Using a pencil, divide each plastic-foam shape into four equal sections. Sections should run up and down the length of the shape.

2 Cover the pencil lines with the wider gold-edged satin ribbon (white satin ribbon for the white/gold ornament; red satin ribbon for the red/gold ornament). Repeat the process with the narrower gold-edged satin ribbon, running it down the middle of the wider ribbon. This creates a strip of ribbon with four gold stripes.

3 Place a row of pearl units (a small pearl bead threaded onto a pin) into the plastic-foam shape along the edges of the ribbon in each of the four blank sections between the ribbon (white pearls for the white/gold ornament; gold pearls for the red/gold ornament).

4 Along the edge of the pearl units, place a row of "cup down" matte gold sequin units.

5 Fill in the remaining blank space with rows of "cup-up" bead and sequin units (clear glass beads and mother-of-pearl sequins for the white/gold ball; red beads and sequins for the red/gold ball).

6 Make a double set of loops over two opposite sequined sections using the gold metallic ribbon.

7 Using the same gold metallic ribbon, make a second set of double loops over the remaining two opposite sequined sections, at right angles to the first.

8 Form a hanging loop and place it on the top of the ornament across the ribbon loops.

9 Decorate and complete the ornament by placing the hat pin units listed below in the center top (over the ribbon loops) and the center bottom.

TOP UNIT

This consists of a teardrop hat pin (white for the white/gold ornament; red for the red/gold ornament) passed through a tiny gold bead, a small crystal cut-glass bead, and a gold filigree cap (convex).

BOTTOM UNIT

This comprises a teardrop hat pin (white for white/gold; red for red/gold) passed through a tiny gold bead, a medium crystal cut-glass bead, a tiny gold bead, a large crystal cut-glass bead, and a gold filigree cap (concave).

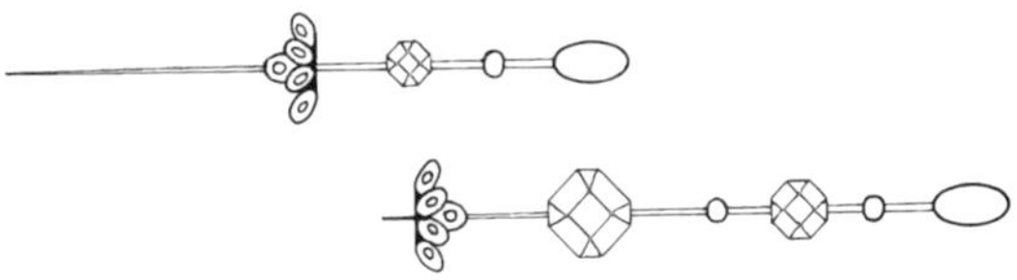

ACCORDIAN ANGELS

MATERIALS

12 inches paper ribbon, approximately
3½ inches wide
Scissors
Rub-on face transfer
Tape measure
4 inches gold glitter chenille (or a 12-inch pipe cleaner, cut into thirds)
18 inches wire
1 head bead, ¾ inch
Doll hair
1 bow, ½–¾ inch
Glue

1 Cut the ribbon into three pieces: one piece measuring 8 inches for the dress, and two pieces measuring 2 inches each for the sleeves.

2 Pleat the three pieces of ribbon accordian-style along their width. Make the pleats ¼ inch wide and 3½ inches long.

3 Place the glitter chenille between folds at the center back of the longer piece of ribbon. Pinch up one end of ribbon around the chenille. Wind one end of wire twice around the ribbon and chenille, about ¼ inch from end of the ribbon.

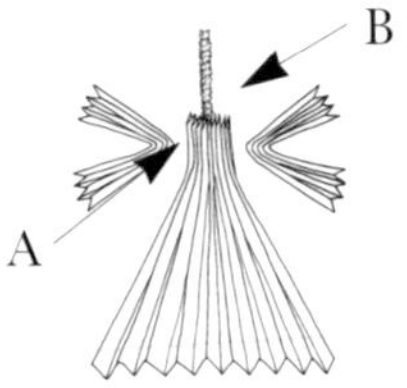

4 Fold small piece of ribbon in half (see diagram) and butt the fold to point "A". Use the wire to bind this sleeve to the chenille, through the center fold. Repeat with the other sleeve at "B". Pull wire around and twist at the back. Use it to attach the angel to the tree.

5 Thread a head bead onto the glitter stem protruding above the dress and sleeves. Push it down until it touches the top edge of ribbon. Use the excess chenille to form a halo by twisting it around your finger, above the head bead. Glue hair onto the head bead, and transfer the face onto the bead, following the manufacturer's directions.

6 Glue a tiny bow over the wire at the front of the angel's dress.

FLUFFY DOUBLE-LOOP BOW

MATERIALS

Scissors
54 inches matte gold paper ribbon, approximately 2 inches wide
36 inches florist's wire
Gold acrylic paint
Paintbrush or sponge

1 Cut two strips of ribbon 8 inches long, and two strips of ribbon 12 inches long, leaving one strip of ribbon 14 inches long.

2 Fold one 8-inch strip of ribbon in half. Scrunch it up along this central line and hold, then form loops with each of the cut ends of the paper strips by overlapping ¼– ½ inch. Wrap the bow with wire. Repeat with the other 8-inch ribbon strip.

3 Place the two sets of loops formed with the 8-inch strips of ribbon side by side. Wire them together, side by side.

4 Repeat steps 2 and 3 with the 12-inch strips of ribbon.

5 Place the small set of ribbon loops over the larger set of ribbon loops. Take the 14-inch

Accordian angel

ribbon strip, scrunch the center, and place it over the middle of the two sets of bow loops. Wrap this strip of ribbon around to the back of the bow loops and tie the ends in a single knot, pulling tightly to hold (you could wire the two sets of ribbon loops together first, if desired).

6 Pull the bow tails down and cut V-shaped notches in the ends. Fluff out the bow loops.

7 Paint the bow very lightly with gold acrylic paint using a paintbrush or sponge.

8 Thread a 6-inch piece of wire through the back of the bow. Use this to attach the bow to the tree, wreath, swag, napkin, or wrapped package.

MINIATURE PRESENTS AND FAVORS

On pages 97 and 99 you will find the directions for making these small gift ornaments and miniature Christmas favors. For my color themes, I have used a gold foil wrapping paper, which has been decorated with ribbon curls made from florist's ribbon. The curls were shredded with a ribbon shredder to make the curls much finer, giving them a more delicate appearance.

CLOTH BALLS

MATERIALS

Molded plastic-foam shapes
Pencil
Tape measure
Tissue paper
Scissors
Christmas fabric, 6 x 3 inches
Glue
40–80 inches ribbon
12 inches lace or braid
Short pins
Long dressmaker's pins
Hat pins, cut crystal beads, and filigree caps

1 Make a paper pattern by dividing the plastic-foam shape into four equal sections. Mark the sections with a pencil and measure them to make sure they are equal. Lay a piece of tissue paper over one section and trace out the pattern from the lines on the plastic-foam. Cut out the pattern and check that it fits. Although this pattern can be used over and over again when covering that particular shape and size of plastic-foam, it is advisable to section off each shape lightly with a pencil before moving on to the next step.

2 Using the pattern, cut out four pieces of fabric for each ornament.

3 Spread a thin line of glue along the inside of the pencil lines all the way around one section. Place a piece of fabric over the glue. Press down the two points of fabric, and then run a finger down the center of the fabric, smoothing it out over the curve of the shape. Ease in the edges of the fabric to prevent tucks appearing. Very tiny tucks along the edge will not show after they have been covered with lace, ribbon, or braid. Glue fabric pieces to the remaining three sections on the plastic-foam shape. As you are working, trim away any fabric that overlaps onto another section. Do not worry about very small gaps between fabric pieces because these can be covered by ribbon, lace. or braid.

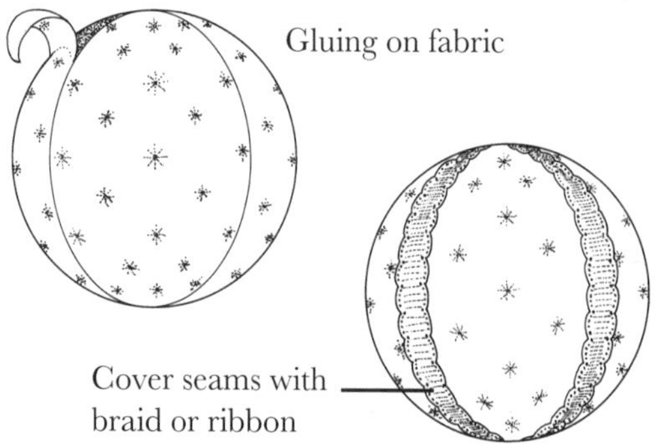

4 Cover the seams between the fabric pieces using lace, ribbon, or braid. Pin them in place at the top and bottom of the shape.

5 There are many ways to decorate the top of this ornament using ribbons. You can form ribbon loops, as shown in steps 5–7, or see alternatives in step 8. To make the ribbon loops, take two long pins and place them so they are firmly secured, yet protruding, about one-third of the way down from the top of the

Opposite *Miniature presents, favors, and cloth balls*

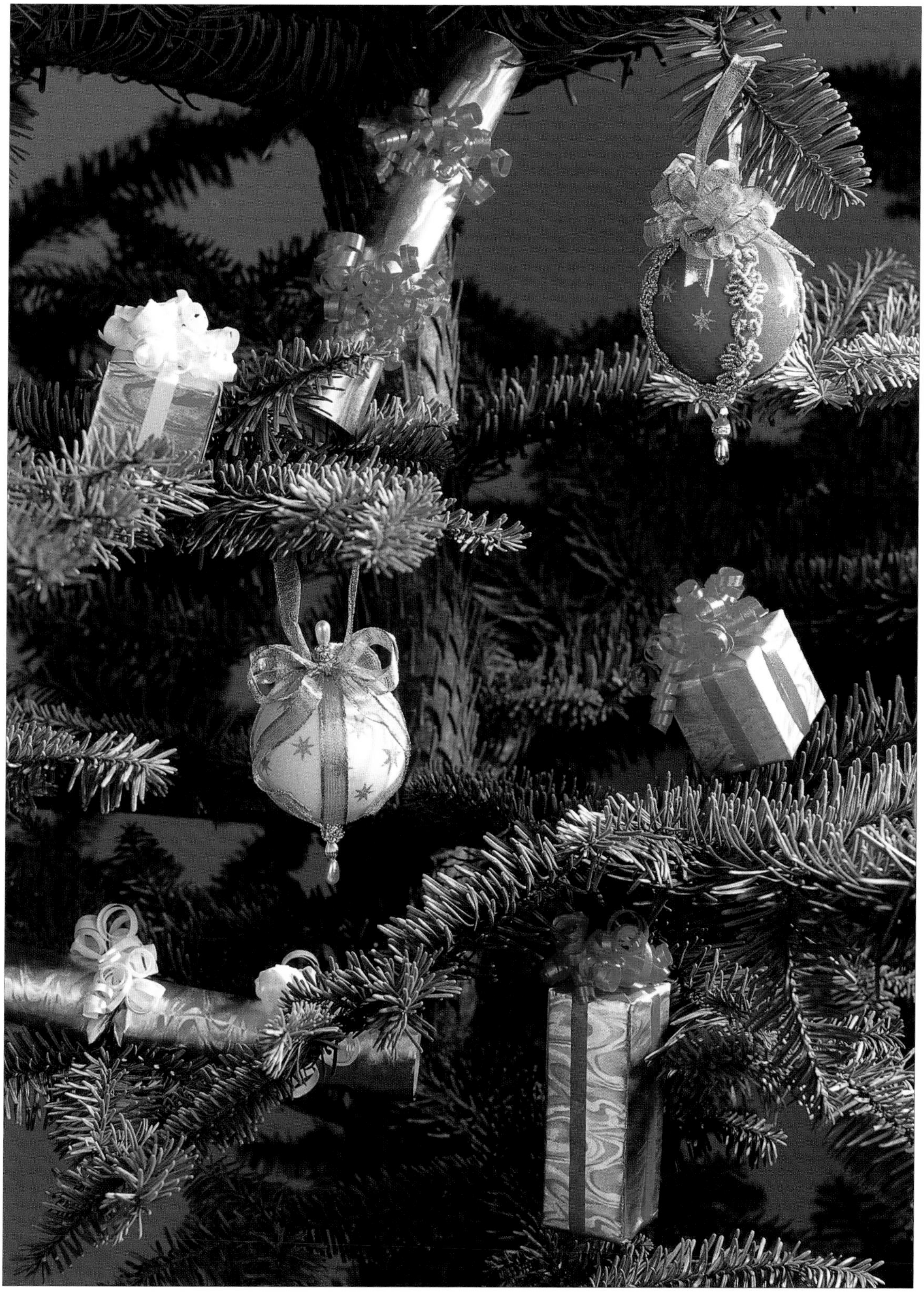

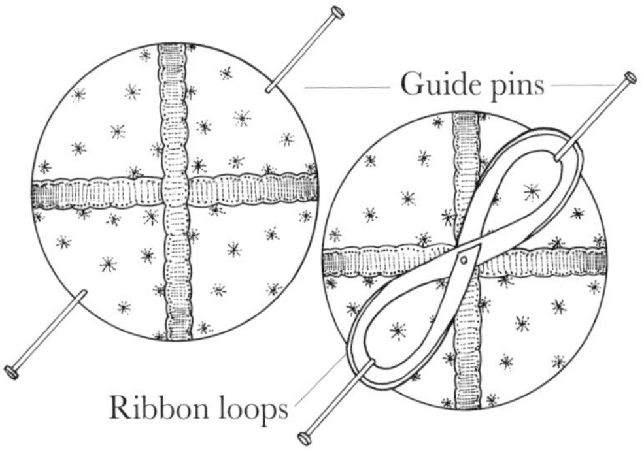

shape on two opposite sides in the center of the section. These are guide pins and are removed after the ribbon loops are completed. Attach one cut end of the ribbon to the center top of the shape. Keep the ribbon flat (do not twist), and wind it clockwise around one guide pin, then back to the beginning. Then wind the ribbon counterclockwise around the other guide pin. Check to see that this figure-of-eight set of loops is of equal length and fullness on both sides. Secure in place with short pins.

6 Make a second set of loops directly over the previous set, but do *not* cut the ribbon. Replace the guide pins ¼ inch closer to the top of the shape. Make another set of loops directly over the first ones, but a little smaller. This can be repeated for more loops.

7 To form a set of loops at right angles to the first set of loops, first cut the ribbon. Start again, this time forming the loops described in step 5 over the other two sections.

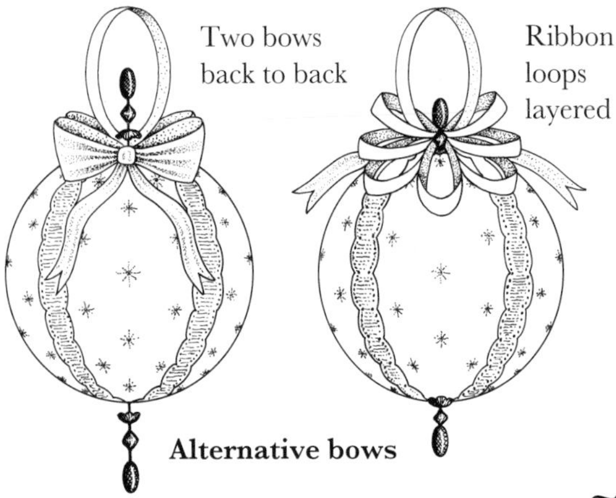

Alternative bows

8 Alternatively, you can tie two simple bows and place them back-to-back, with the hanging loop from step 9 placed between them. You could also stack several layers of bow loops to form a pom-pom bow with the hanging loop extending from the top of the bow.

9 To form a hanging loop, take 6–8 inches of ribbon and form a large loop, overlapping the two cut ends. Using short pins, attach the cut ends at the top center of the ornament, between the ribbon loops.

10 Now decorate the top and bottom of the ornament with a hat pin passed through a cut crystal bead and a filigree cap, or your choice of jewelry findings. These will cover any pins or cut ends of the ribbons.

GEMSTONE ORNAMENTS

MATERIALS

Papier-mâché ornaments (stars, hearts, bells, etc.)
Gold acrylic paint
Paintbrush
Glue
Flat-backed artificial gemstones
Gold cord and braids

1 Paint the papier-mâché shapes with two or more coats of gold acrylic paint, leaving the paint to dry thoroughly between coats.

2 Decorate the papier-mâché shapes by gluing on gemstones, cord, and braid. For example, you could use the cord or braid to divide the ornament into sections, which you can then decorate with gemstones. Use your imaginative skills to make creative designs.

Opposite *Gemstone ornaments*

Table Setting

Gold reflects a lavish brilliance and richness in both the red and the white table settings. Elegant beaded linen, using a simple but classic poinsettia design, forms the background to the splendid golden centerpiece. The stylish Italian candy favor, filled with enticing handmade chocolates, makes an exquisite focus to a very sophisticated dinner table.

Gold and white table setting

The Wreath

5 Place the candle in the center of the urn. Pack dry florist's compound around the candle and up to the rim of the urn to secure it.

6 Place the artichokes on each side of the candle, toward the front of the urn.

7 Place one bunch of plums at the front of the candle, between the two artichokes. Place the other two bunches behind the candle, spaced an equal distance apart.

8 Place one twig branch in the front of the arrangement, between the plums and the candle. Place the other two branches toward

the back of the arrangement, behind the artichokes.

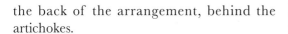

9 Make a simple looped bow using a 30-inch piece of wired ribbon. Fold it in half to find the center, and scrunch this together along the width of the ribbon, point A.

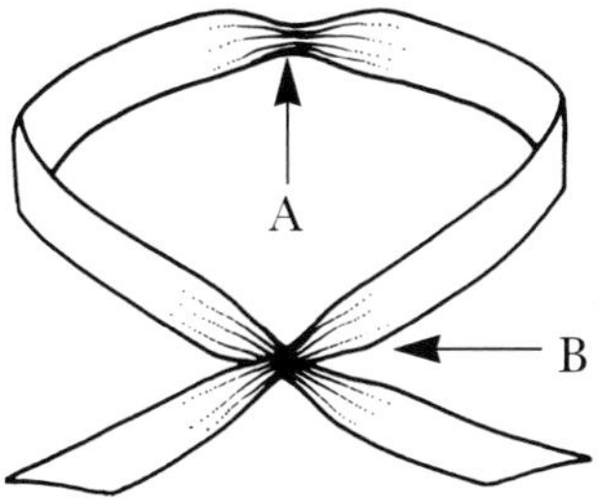

Measure 8 inches from each end, overlap and scrunch along the width of the ribbon, point B. Bring together points A and B, and wrap firmly with florist's wire. Twist the ends together to form a tail to poke into the arrangement.

10 Place the simple looped bow at the front of the arrangement, in the gap between the plums and the twig branch.

11 Fill in the gaps and spaces around the arrangement with saligmum and bunches of leaves. Fill any gaps close to the edge of the urn with moss.

Room Decorations

A Christmas wreath makes a simple but elegant decoration for any door. I have chosen a thick golden cord, which is twisted among the lush evergreen branches. Striking bows with furled tails form the focal point, and these are accented by miniature presents and favors.

THE WREATH

MATERIALS

Premade evergreen wreath
2 yards gold cord
Florist's wire
4 Fluffy double-loop bows (see page 10)
2 Miniature favors (see page 99)
2 Gift ornaments (see page 97)

1 Starting from the back of the wreath, weave gold cord in and out of the branches, all around the wreath. Secure the ends in place with small pieces of florist's wire. To make the cord even more secure, attach it to the branches at regular intervals with wire.

2 Attach four fluffy double-loop bows to the wreath with florist's wire, spacing them evenly. Make sure that the florist's wire is concealed behind the branches of the wreath.

3 Decorate the remaining gaps on the wreath with a few of the miniature favors and gift ornaments used on the Christmas tree, wiring them neatly in position.

CHAPTER 3

A Tartan Theme

IN RECENT YEARS the use of various Scottish tartans has become more popular in interior home decor. The combination of rich red, deep green, and burnished gold in the form of a bold plaid pattern lends itself perfectly to a cozy Christmas theme.

The same plaid fabric, made into lovely bows, is used repeatedly to provide fresh and luxuriant color, not only on this Yuletide tree but throughout the chapter's decorations. Perfectly shaped bows with ruched tails can be found on the wreath at the front door, within the branches of the fireplace swag, adorning the wine basket, and mounted on the back of the Golden Swan Centerpiece (see page 54).

The tartan theme lends itself perfectly as a backdrop to many other themes. You could add a collection of ornaments to reflect a special personal or family preference, or include artificial apples, oranges, and plums to complement the setting. Regardless of your heritage, the Scottish tartan makes an attractive theme.

Tree Decorations

For this tartan theme, I have chosen a mixture of natural textures and brilliant metals, which are woven together by a profusion of lush plaid fabric. The Christmas evergreen reflects this blend of rugged simplicity in nature, as depicted by the Pinecone Angel and Bird in a Nest ornaments (see page 42). Bundles of heather tied together with satin ribbons, along with dried thistles, lend authenticity, while miniature boxes and Christmas favors add gaiety to the earthy somberness.

STIFFENED TREE BOWS

MATERIALS

Scissors
1 yard Christmas plaid fabric, 45 inches wide (makes about 18 bows)
Aluminum foil
Adhesive tape
Fabric stiffener
Coat hangers and clothespins
Iron
90-gauge wire
Low-temperature glue gun and glue sticks
Soft plastic wrap, for stuffing
Craft shellac or water-based glaze
Paintbrush

1 For each bow, cut the following strips of fabric: 1 long streamer piece—3 x 13 inches; 1 bow loop piece—3 x 14 inches; and 1 connector piece—½ x 4 inches.

2 Lay the aluminum foil down flat on your work surface. Secure it in place with adhesive tape, around the edges if possible, making sure that it is taut. Place the streamer piece on top of the foil with the right side of the fabric facing upward.

3 Pour a small amount of fabric stiffener down the center of the fabric. Spread it over the entire piece with your fingers. Turn the fabric over and repeat on the wrong side. Repeat this process with the bow loop piece and the connector piece for all the bows.

4 Using clothespins, hang all the pieces of fabric by a short end (not in the middle), on coat hangers. Let them dry thoroughly.

5 When completely dry, remove the pieces from the hanger and run a medium-hot iron over both sides of one set of pieces—streamer, bow loops, and connector. Work with just one set of strips at a time. The heat will make the stiffened fabric more flexible. Bows should be formed while the pieces are soft.

6 To form the bow, fold the streamer piece in half along its length, to determine the center. Form two or three small pleats across the width at the center; hold with a clothespin.

7 Place the bow loop piece onto the work surface with the wrong side of the fabric facing upward. Find the center and bring the ends of the strip together, overlapping the center and each other by at least ½ inch. Gather the folded strip in the center with

three pleats, as with the streamer piece. Hold in place with a clothespin.

8 To assemble, place the bow loops over the streamer, matching pleated centers. Place an 8-inch wire (90-gauge) along the back side of the streamer. The wire is used to attach bows to the tree. Tightly wrap the connector strip twice around the bow loops, streamer, and wire. Glue in place using a low-temperature hot glue gun.

9 Stuff each of the bow loops carefully with balls of plastic wrap to shape them. Trim the streamers to the desired length, cutting V-shaped notches in the ends.

10 Paint the bow with two thin layers of craft shellac to seal and protect it. When dry, remove the balls of plastic wrap and paint the inside of the loops with a coat of the shellac.

Stiffened tree bow and miniature favors (page 42)

MINIATURE PRESENTS AND FAVORS

For the gift boxes, follow the directions given on page 97 for making present ornaments. For this tartan theme, I have used matte paper in red or green and decorated the little boxes with raffia tied into small bows.

For the Christmas favors, follow the directions given on page 99. I made several, using recycled paper in two different colors—a rustic red and a somber green to echo the more traditional mood of the plaid tree. To add extra brightness, you could use plaid foil in the same colors as the tree bows. The favors were then decorated with raffia tied around each end.

PINECONE ANGEL

MATERIALS

Low-temperature glue gun and glue sticks
1 medium-sized acorn with cap
1 pinecone, 4–6 inches long
3–4 inches natural brown paper wire
1 small sprig green moss
1 piece dried brown leaf
6 inches dark green satin ribbon, $^{1}/_{16}$ inch wide
Small white cedar cones
2 dried milkweed pods
3 inches fine wire

1 Glue the acorn to the top of the pinecone, with the bottom facing toward the front and pointing down slightly.

2 Fold the cut ends of the paper wire back. Tuck the center of the wire in between the petals on the cone, about 1 inch above the stem. Bend the open ends of the wire toward the center front to form hands.

3 Glue the moss in between the hands, then glue a dried leaf over the moss.

4 Cut the ribbon in half and form two loops. Overlap them and glue them over the leaf. Glue on the white cedar cones.

5 Glue the two pods to the center of the back of the pinecone to form wings. Glue a small wire loop at the back for the hanger.

BIRD IN A NEST

MATERIALS

Scissors
Tape measure
1 yard red satin ribbon, $^{1}/_{4}$ inch wide
Low-temperature glue gun and glue sticks
1 small nest-shaped basket, 2-3 inches in diameter
Cloth-covered wire
Red raffia
2 stems green moss
1 small artificial (mushroom) bird
Baby's breath

1 Cut two 7 inch pieces of ribbon. Turn all cut ends under and glue the ends of the ribbons to the sides of the basket so they crisscross over the basket.

2 Gather the ribbon tightly with wire at the top where the ribbons cross over. With the remaining ribbon, form a double-loop bow and glue this to the wired ribbon.

3 Fill the nest with raffia. Glue green moss to the nest in one section between the two ribbons. Add the bird and attach a small piece of raffia to the bird's beak. Glue baby's breath to the moss to add little highlights.

Opposite *Pinecone angel, bird in a nest, and miniature present*

Room Decorations

To extend the tartan theme throughout your home, why not make some of the exciting projects in this section. Hang a Christmas swag decorated with pinecones, ornaments, and plaid bows over your mantelpiece, or enliven your dining room with a wine basket painted green and decorated with a festive plaid bow. Traditionalists may prefer to make a Christmas stocking and decorate it with one of the colorful ideas in this section. Alternatively, you can make a wreath arrangement from evergreen, holly, plaid bows and a splendid french horn to complete the look.

FRENCH HORN SWAG

MATERIALS

Homemade swag (see pages 106–107)
Florist's wire
6 Stiffened tree bows (see page 40)
Low-temperature glue gun and glue sticks (optional)
Assorted pinecones
French horn wreath (see page 49)
8 Pinecone angel ornaments (see page 42)
8 Miniature presents (see page 97)
8 Miniature favors (see page 99)

1 Hang your preferred-style homemade swag in position on the mantelpiece. Referring to the photograph above for guidance, wire a stiffened tree bow into each of the outer corners of the swag. Be careful to conceal the wire in the branches of the swag. Wire or glue pinecones of various shapes and sizes to form a cluster above each bow.

French horn swag and wine basket (page 46)

2 Wire the French horn wreath in the middle of the swag (if a nail or hook is holding up the swag, hang and wire the French horn to this). Attach one stiffened tree bow to the swag, halfway between the centerpiece and the outside corner. Attach another bow halfway down the tail of the swag. Repeat on the other side of the swag.

3 Wire the pinecone angels, and miniature presents and favors, in between the bows.

4 Attach as many other pinecones, bows, and ornaments as space allows.

WINE BASKET

MATERIALS

Divided wine basket
Christmas green spray paint
Paintbrush
Gold acrylic paint
Scissors
½ yard Christmas plaid fabric, 36 or 45 inches wide
Tape measure
Aluminum foil
Adhesive tape
Fabric stiffener
Coat hanger and clothespins
Low-temperature glue gun and glue sticks
Soft plastic wrap, for stuffing
Craft shellac or water-based glaze

1 In a well-ventilated area, spray the basket with several light coats of green spray paint. Allow the paint to dry thoroughly between coats.

2 Using a paintbrush, paint the rim of the basket with two coats of gold acrylic paint, letting the first coat dry before applying the second.

3 Cut the fabric into three strips, in the following sizes:
1 streamer piece—8 x 30 inches;
1 bow loop piece—8 x 18 inches;
1 connector piece—4 x 10 inches.

4 Follow the simple directions given for making a stiffened bow, as in steps 2–14 on pages 49–50.

5 Glue the bow into position at the front of the basket, or wherever desired.

Opposite *Christmas stockings*

CHRISTMAS STOCKINGS

MATERIALS

Felt in coordinating color, 24 x 16 inches
Scissors
Plaid fabric, 1 yard x 14 inches
Tape measure
Fusible web
Iron
Needle and thread
Ribbon for a hanger

MAKING A STOCKING

1 Enlarge the pattern on pages 122-123 by 150 percent. Fold the felt in half to form a piece measuring 12 x 16 inches. Next, cut two enlarged, full stocking patterns from the felt. One piece will form the front, and one piece will form the back of the stocking. From the plaid fabric, cut one piece measuring 14½ x 10 inches for the contrasting stocking top, and two pieces each of the contrasting toe and heel pieces. From the fusible web, cut two pieces each of the toe and the heel, about ⅛ inch smaller all around than the enlarged pattern.

2 Using an iron on a warm setting, apply the fusible web to the wrong side of the plaid toe and heel fabric pieces, following the manufacturer's directions. Then apply the plaid heel and toe pieces to the right sides of the felt stocking pieces, both on the front and the back.

3 Decorate the front stocking piece as desired (see ideas on page 48).

4 Place the two felt stocking pieces together, with wrong sides facing. Stitch around the outside of the pieces, ⅛ inch from the cut edge, leaving the top open.

2 Follow the directions given for making a stiffened bow, as in steps 2–11 on pages 49–50. Coat the ring piece with fabric stiffener, and fold in the same way as the other strips.

3 Take the ring piece and form a circle with at least a ½ inch overlap. Gather the overlapped section with three pleats, similar to the streamer and bow loop pieces. Hold in place with a clothespin.

4 To assemble, stack the bow loop piece over the streamer piece, matching the pleated centers. Glue together using the low-temperature glue gun. Stack the bow and streamer piece over the ring piece, and glue in place with hot glue. Glue one end of the connector piece to the inside of the ring piece, under the overlapping section of fabric. Tightly wrap the connector piece around all three layers (streamer, bow, and ring) two or three times. Bond the connector piece to the inside of the ring piece with low-temperature hot glue. Trim any surplus from the connector piece.

5 Open up the bow loops and stuff both the ring and bow loops with balls of plastic wrap. When dry, trim the streamers to the desired length, making V-shaped notches.

6 When completely dry, remove the stuffing and paint the bow with two coats of craft shellac to seal and protect the fabric.

GOLDEN SWAN CENTERPIECE

MATERIALS

Papier-mâché swan (available from craft stores)
Gold spray paint
Paintbrush
Gold acrylic paint
Scissors
1 yard Christmas plaid fabric, 45 inches wide
Tape measure
Craft shellac or water-based glaze
Aluminum foil
Adhesive tape
Fabric stiffener
Coat hanger and clothespins
Low-temperature glue gun and glue sticks
Soft plastic wrap, for stuffing
Small pieces of evergreen
Sprigs of heather
Sprigs of baby's breath

1 In a well-ventilated area, spray the swan with two light coats of gold spray paint. Alternatively, use a paintbrush to paint the swan with two coats of gold acrylic paint.

2 Cut the fabric into three strips for the bow, as follows:
1 streamer piece – 8 x 45 inches;
1 bow loop piece – 8 x 18 inches;
1 connector piece – 4 x 10 inches.

3 From the remaining fabric, cut out motifs to appliqué onto the swan. (Study the photograph on pages 52-53)

4 Using the craft shellac, stick the appliqué motifs into the desired positions around the swan. Leave to dry, then brush on one or two coats of craft shellac.

5 Make a bow following the directions for making a stiffened bow, as given in steps 2–14 on pages 49–50.

6 Glue the bow into position at the back of the swan with the tails furled out behind.

7 Glue small pieces of fresh, preserved, or silk evergreen along the back of the swan so they extend out from the bow, between the two furled tails. Add a few sprigs of heather and baby's breath to the arrangement.

TARTAN FAVORS

Materials

Recycled matte wrapping paper, 13½ x 8 inches
A printed joke, saying, verse, or fortune
Cardboard, 7 x 3¾ inches
Glue
2 cylinders (plastic piping, 2 inches in diameter), 10 inches long and 6 inches long
Waxed cord
Party hat and small gifts
16 inches plaid ribbon, 1½ inches wide
1½ yard gold-edged satin ribbon, ¼ inch wide

1 Referring to the diagram on page 99 for positioning, put the paper right side down on the work surface. Place the printed joke in the center of the paper. Place the cardboard along the bottom edge. Spread glue along the top edge of the paper.

2 With the long cylinder on the left and the short cylinder on the right, butt the ends of the tubes along the right-hand edge of the cardboard. Roll the paper around them, holding them together, until reaching the glued edge. Continue to roll over the glued edge. Wipe away any excess glue and leave to dry.

3 Pull the short cylinder on the right about ¾ inch away from the right-hand edge of the stiff card ("pull line A" on the diagram). Wrap the waxed cord twice around the paper, centrally between the right-hand edge of the cardboard and the left-hand edge of the short cylinder ("cord line A" on the diagram).

4 Pull the ends of the waxed cord in opposite directions, so the cord creases the paper around the edge of the cardboard. Push the short tube back against the longer tube and the cardboard to shape the favor. Remove the cord, then the short tube.

5 Into the remaining long tube, drop a folded party hat and a few little gifts. Carefully pull the long tube to "pull line B." Make sure that the gifts drop into the favor before closing the other end.

6 Wrap the cord twice around the paper at "cord line B." Pull the cord tightly, as in step 4. Push the long tube tube back against the cardboard. Remove the cord and the tube.

7 Cut the plaid ribbon into two. Gather up each piece along one long edge to make a ruffle and tie one in each crease. Glue satin ribbon around the outside edges and in the central section. Tie two bows with the remaining satin ribbon; glue one over each plaid ruffle.

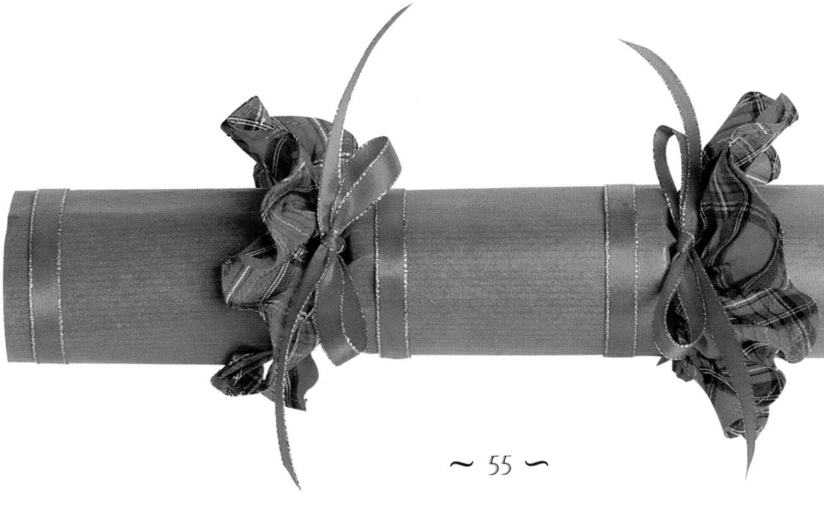

CHAPTER 4

A Toyland Theme

PREPARING FOR CHRISTMAS can be particularly fun and satisfying when decorating the tree and home for younger family members. Children love to make things and have a special appreciation for handmade creations. Maybe the reason why adults love the seasonal preparations is because it reminds them of the wonderful time they had when they were children!

One of the nice things about our toyland theme is the ease with which it can be incorporated into any other theme — color, country, Victorian, and so on. All you have to do is add toys and novelties to correspond with the particular theme. For example, you could add cornhusk dolls and miniature scarecrows in the country theme. For the Victorian theme, you might add small vintage toys from that era, such as spinning tops and china dolls. It is so much fun to design and create this festive theme, and the final result always delights young and old alike.

Tree Decorations

For the toyland tree, I have chosen the basic Christmas colors of red, white and green. To light the tree, I have used multicolored miniature bulbs. Garlands of everlasting candies swing from the tree boughs, which are dotted with frosted cookies and lollipops. Colorful hobby horses and dressed-up teddy bears guard the birthday cake candles in specially decorated spools, which are for decoration only. Miniature gifts hint at the anticipated exchange of presents on Christmas morning, when we all become kids at heart!

CANDY GARLAND

MATERIALS

The amount of materials required depends on the number and length of garlands you are making. The amounts given below will make one 25-inch garland. For my tree, I used eight garlands of this length.

16 squares of assorted fabric, 4 x 4 inches
16 cotton balls
Dressmaker's pins
32 lengths of wire, approximately 8 inches long
Needle-nose pliers
32 lengths of ribbon, 10–12 inches long, to coordinate with the fabric

1 Taking one square of fabric at a time, unravel two opposite edges to form a fringe about ¼ inch wide.

2 Place a fabric square on a work surface so the wrong side is facing upward and the fringed edges are on the left and right sides.

3 Place a cotton ball at the bottom (non fringed) edge of the fabric square, centrally between the two fringed edges. Fold ½ inch of the top edge of the fabric toward the cotton ball. Then roll the fabric along the bottom edge around the cotton ball toward the opposite nonfringed edge, to form a tube. Hold the fabric in place with a pin.

4 Wrap a piece of wire around each side of the cotton ball, approximately 1 inch from each of the fringed edges. Wrap the wire around twice and pull tightly (using needle-nosed pliers can help with pulling the wire tight). Twist the two wires together two or three times to complete the candy shape. Remove the pin. Repeat to make 15 more candy shapes. Do not trim the wire.

5 Place the wired sections of two candies over each other at an angle. Wrap and twist the excess wire around to the back (where the fold is) to attach them to each other. Repeat this process until you have 16 candies attached in a garland chain.

6 Leave the wire on the two ends of the chain to attach the garland to the tree. Trim the remaining wires at the back of the garland chain and, using pliers, tuck the wire ends under the folded edge of the fabric.

7 Tie small ribbon bows with the pieces of ribbon, and glue these over the wires at the front of the garland chain.

TREE SKIRT

An easy way of finishing off the area around the bottom of the tree is with a tree skirt. Plain fabric tree skirts can be purchased quite inexpensively; for directions on how to make one, see page 88. Once the basic skirt is made, you can decorate it in many different ways. For the toyland tree skirt, I used the same candy garland that is used on the tree. A chain of 86 candy-shaped pieces are joined together in a chain, which is then basted around a plain white tree skirt (making it easy to remove to wash or to alter the decoration).

WRAPPED LOLLIPOP

MATERIALS

Measurements given are per lollipop, and may need to be adjusted depending on the size of lollipop used.

Christmas fabric, 4½ inches square
Tulle, 5½ inches square
Lollipop
7–8 inches craft wire (28-gauge)
12 inches satin ribbon

1 Unravel the threads along all the edges of the Christmas fabric square to form a fringe about ¼ inch wide.

Candy garland and wrapped lollipops

2 Place the fabric square down on a work surface with the wrong side facing up. Place the tulle centrally over the fabric, and place the lollipop in the center of the tulle.

3 Pulling the corners up first, wrap the fabric around the lollipop, using wire to hold it in place around the lollipop stick. Leave 1½–2 inches of the wire ends for attaching the lollipop to the tree branches.

4 Tie ribbon around the wire (leave wire ends to attach to tree), and tie a simple bow at the opposite side to the wire ends.

PRESENT ORNAMENTS

These delightful little boxes are so quick and easy to make and to decorate that you will soon find yourself making dozens to adorn your tree each year (find the directions on pages 97–98). For the toyland theme, I have used red and green recycled paper with florist's ribbon curls to decorate the advent gifts.

Present ornaments and hobby horse

HOBBY HORSE

Materials

Tracing paper
Pencil
Fabric A, 5 x 10 inches
Fabric B, 11 x 3 inches
Scissors
Felt, 2 x 3 inches
Needle and thread
Pins
25 inches satin ribbon (in a coordinating color), $^1/_8$ inch wide
5-inch wooden dowel, $^1/_4$ inch thick
Glue
Batting or toy stuffing
Strong thread
4 small buttons in colors to coordinate with fabric
2 large buttons

1 Trace the hobby horse head and ear patterns (see page 122). Position the head tracing over fabric A and cut out two pieces. Position the tracing of the ears over the felt and cut out two.

2 Fold fabric B in half lengthwise, with right sides together, making it 11 x 1$^1/_2$ inches. Sew a $^1/_4$-inch seam along the width at each end of the folded strip. Turn right sides out and press. Sew a gathering stitch along the raw edges. Pull the gathering threads until the fabric measures approximately 5 inches. This will be the "mane" piece.

3 Place one end of the mane piece $^1/_4$ inch from the bottom outside edge of one head piece, right sides together. Pin the remainder of the mane piece along the outside edge of that head piece (see the diagram).

4 With the right sides of the head pieces together, sew together (through the mane), leaving an $^1/_8$-inch seam allowance. Leave an opening at the bottom of the head, as indicated on the pattern.

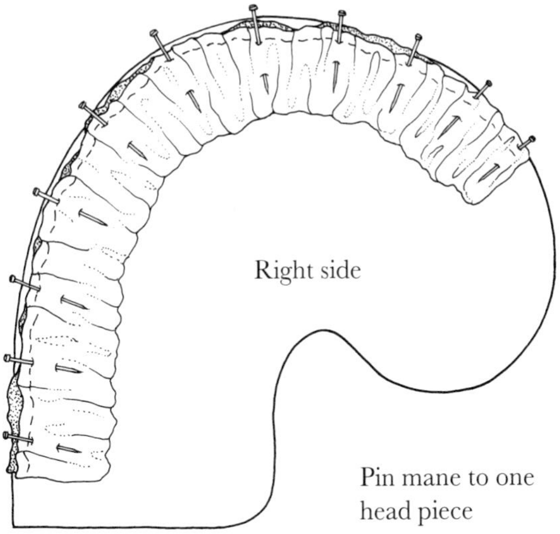

5 Wrap satin ribbon spirally around the wooden dowel. Secure the ribbon at each end with a dab of glue.

6 Turn the head piece right side out and stuff it lightly with batting. Place the dowel into the neck and continue stuffing around the dowel. Hand-stitch the bottom of the neck.

7 Fold one ear in half lengthwise and oversew the bottom edge. Repeat with the other ear. Stitch the ears into place on each side of the head.

8 Using very strong thread, stitch buttons to the head to form eyes. Pull the buttons in very tightly, to form small indentations.

9 Place satin ribbon around the nose and head to form the halter. Glue ribbon reins to the halter.

10 Glue one large button on each side of the bottom end of the dowel to form wheels. Glue a small button in the center of each of the larger buttons.

SPOOL CANDLESTICK

MATERIALS

The amount of materials are approximate and depend on the size of spool used. Other colors of paint and ribbon may be used, as wished.

Wooden thread spools
White gloss acrylic paint
Paintbrush
Miniature clothespin (available from craft stores and doll-making suppliers)
Green gloss acrylic paint
Glue
15 inches Christmas green satin ribbon, 1/16 inch wide
3 inches Christmas red satin ribbon, 1/16 inch wide
2 inches red rose trim
Low-temperature hot glue gun and glue sticks
Red birthday cake candle
12 inches white satin ribbon, 1/16 inch wide

1 Paint the wooden spool with white gloss acrylic paint, and paint the miniature clothespin with green gloss acrylic paint. Let dry, before applying a second coat, if necessary.

2 Glue green ribbon around the top of the spool, red ribbon around the bottom and the red rose trim around the center of the spool.

3 Almost fill the hole at the green ribbon end of the spool with hot glue and quickly attach a candle, holding it in place until the glue cools.

4 Tie a double bow with the white satin and remaining green satin ribbons, and glue it to the bottom of the candle where it enters the spool.

5 Using the hot glue gun, glue the miniature clothespin to the bottom of the spool. Use the clothespin to attach the candlestick to the tree.

CAUTION: These candles and candlesticks are for decoration only, and should not be lit under any circumstances.

SANTA'S TEDDY HELPER

MATERIALS

Scissors
Red felt, 4 x 3 1/2 inches
White felt, 1 1/2 x 4 inches
Glue
Needle and thread
1 white pompom, 3/8 inch in diameter
2 red pompoms, 3/8 inch in diameter
Jointed teddy bear, 4 inches long
Red felt or ribbon, 8 x 1/4 inches

1 Following the pattern given on page 122, cut out one hat pattern from the 4 x 3 1/2-inch piece of red felt. Cut the cuff pattern from the white felt.

2 Glue the white felt cuff piece to the bottom edge of the red felt hat piece, as indicated by the dotted line on the pattern.

3 Fold the hat in half lengthwise, sew an 1/8-inch seam, turn inside out, and press. Stitch a white pompom to the tip of the hat.

4 Place the hat over one ear of the teddy bear and stitch it into place. Bend the hat down, as shown in the photograph.

5 Sew a pompom to each end of the remaining piece of red felt. Tie this around the neck of the teddy bear to make a scarf.

TEDDY WITH VEST

MATERIALS

Tracing paper
Pencil
Scissors
Red or green felt, 8 x 4 inches
Jointed teddy bear, 6 inches long
3 very small buttons, or $^1/_8$-inch beads
Needle and thread
Glue
Christmas fabric for bow tie

1 Trace the pattern given on page 123 and use this to cut out the vest from the felt. Carefully slit the armholes as marked. Cut one strip measuring $^5/_8$ x 2 inches from the Christmas fabric.

2 Slip the felt vest onto the teddy bear. Overlap the right side over the left by about $^1/_4$ inch. Stitch buttons or beads through both layers of the felt to close the vest.

3 Tie a knot in the Christmas fabric strip and trim the ends to form a little bow tie, $^3/_4$ inch long. Glue the bow tie under the teddy's chin and glue a button or bead over the knot.

Spool candlestick, Santa's teddy helper, and the teddy with vest

COOKIE CUTTER ORNAMENTS

Double Heart Cookie Cutter

Materials

Glue
28 inches red polka-dot satin ribbon, $^3/_8$ inch wide
Large heart cookie cutter
Small heart cookie cutter
8 inches red polka-dot satin ribbon, $^1/_8$ inch wide
Jingle bell, $^1/_2$ inch
Scissors
1 red ribbon rose
Low-temperature hot glue gun and glue sticks

1 Glue the wider ribbon centrally around the side of each of the cookie cutters. Trim the excess ribbon away.

2 Thread the narrower ribbon through the bell. Glue the ribbon to the top of the small heart, letting the bell hang slightly inside the smaller heart. Trim the ribbon.

3 Using the narrower ribbon, form a small loop from the large heart to the small heart, letting the small heart hang from the larger heart. Glue the ribbon at the top of the larger heart. Trim the excess ribbon away.

4 With the remaining narrower ribbon, make a hanging loop for the ornament, and glue it to the larger cookie cutter.

5 Cut the remaining wider ribbon in half and form two figure-of-eight shapes. Place one over the top of the other at right angles and glue a ribbon rose in the center. Glue this to the top of the ornament.

Opposite *Double heart, plaid heart, and star cookie cutter ornaments, and frosted cookies (page 66)*

Plaid Heart

Materials

Glue
1 medium heart cookie cutter
7 inches plaid ribbon, $^5/_8$ inch wide
Jingle bell, $^1/_2$ inch
5 inches dark green satin ribbon, $^1/_{16}$ inch wide
Low-temperature hot glue gun and glue sticks
7 inches red feather-edged satin ribbon, $^1/_4$ inch wide
Small green button

1 Spread glue evenly on the outside edge of the cookie cutter. Starting at the top where the heart dips, place the plaid ribbon over the glue, all around the heart shape. Trim away any excess ribbon.

2 Thread the bell onto the narrow green ribbon and suspend it from the center of the heart by making a loop. Use the hot glue gun to glue on the loop.

3 Tie a bow with the red feather-edged ribbon and glue it to the top of the heart. Finish by gluing a small button in the center of the bow.

Star Cookie Cutter

Materials

12 inches red satin ribbon, $^1/_8$ inch wide
Large six-pointed star cookie cutter, 3 inches from point to opposite point
Glue
12 inches feather-edged red satin ribbon, $^3/_8$ inch wide
Ribbon rose

1 Wrap the narrow red ribbon over the star cutter from one inside point (bottom of star point) to the one directly opposite it. Take the

ribbon over the edge and glue it about midway onto the side of the cutter. Repeat to wrap all inside points of the star. The ribbons will intersect in the center.

2 Glue the feather-edged ribbon around the outside edge of the cookie cutter, covering the ends of the narrow ribbon glued to the side.

3 Use 2–2 1/8 inches of narrow red ribbon to make a hanging loop. Form the ribbon into a small loop and glue it to the outside edge of the cutter, in one of the dips between points.

4 Embellish the star ornament by gluing a ribbon rose over the center.

FROSTED COOKIES

MATERIALS

Makes about 50 cookies, depending on size.

1 1/2 cups confectioner's sugar
1 cup softened butter
Mixing bowl
Wooden spoon
1 teaspoon vanilla extract
1/2 teaspoon almond extract
1 egg
1 1/2 cups all-purpose flour
1 teaspoon baking soda
Rolling pin
Cookie cutters
Skewer or toothpick
Baking sheet

Vanilla Frosting:
3 cups confectioner's sugar
1/3 cup softened butter
1 1/2 teaspoons vanilla extract
1-2 tablespoons milk
Food coloring (optional)
Wire rack
Metal spatula
Lengths of ribbon for hanging

1 In a mixing bowl, cream the confectioner's sugar and butter together. When well blended, add vanilla and almond extract, and the egg, mixing well. Slowly add the remaining ingredients, combining thoroughly. Refrigerate for about four hours.

2 Preheat the oven to 350°F. Roll out the dough to a thickness of 1/4 inch and cut out the cookies using decorative cookie cutters. Make a small hole at the top of each cookie with a skewer or toothpick (for threading through the hanging loop later). Bake for 6 to 8 minutes, or until the edges are golden. Let cool on a wire rack.

3 To make the vanilla frosting, cream together the sugar and butter. Gradually stir in the vanilla extract and 1 tablespoon of the milk. Combine thoroughly.

4 Add food coloring, if using. If necessary, add extra milk, one drop or two at a time, until the frosting is smooth and spreadable.

5 When the cookies are cool, spread the frosting over the tops of the cookies with a spatula. Allow to set.

6 Thread a ribbon through the hole at the top of each cookie, knot the ends, and hang the frosted cookies from the tree.

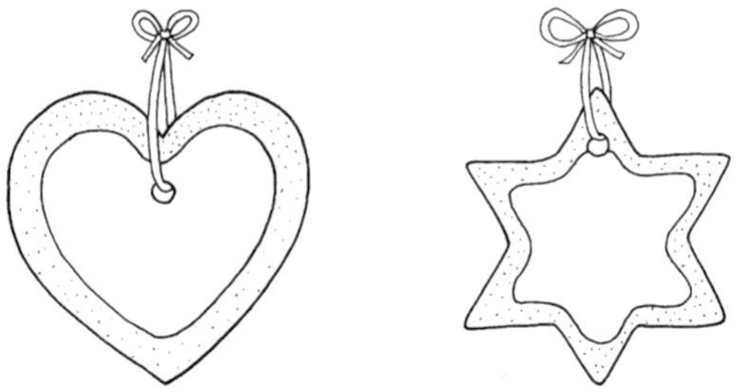

until the paper creases and the cardboard edges touch. Tie the ribbon in a knot, but do not trim the ribbon tails (these will be used to attach the ribbon curls later). Repeat with the other half of the favor.

6 Take ten 18-inch strips of curling ribbon and tie them tightly in the gap between the favor sections. To curl the ribbon, hold one strip of ribbon at a time, as close to the central knot as possible, between your thumb and the sharp edge of a pair of scissors. Pull your thumb and scissor blade firmly to the end of the strip to form a curl. Repeat, holding the strip even tighter if a tighter curl is preferred. Before going on to the next strip of ribbon, use a ribbon shredder to make the curls thinner, giving them a delicate look. Curl and shred the ends of ribbon that formed the knot.

7 Place both favor halves in the center of the table. Fill with shredded paper and arrange candy and presents to look as if the favor has just been pulled and everything is tumbling out.

CHAPTER 5

A Scandinavian Theme

CHRISTMAS IN SCANDINAVIA began as a pagan holiday that was celebrated around January 13th, for three days and nights. In the early 1800s the mixture of Scandinavian tradition and German custom began to form today's celebration.

The festivities begin on Christmas Eve and continue over the next two days with a variety of local customs and traditions. Reciting the Christmas story and singing carols around the tree are as much a part of any Scandinavian Christmas as the festive meals.

Long winter evenings provide time to create the decorations, which form the basis of the various seasonal customs. Woven hearts, sheaves of wheat, beautiful embroidered linens, and a profusion of candles (recreated with electric candle lights) join the snowy white and rosy red festive colors to create that special glow.

Tree Decorations

Focal to the tree is the traditional flag garland, which runs vertically and includes flags from Norway, Sweden, and Denmark. Electric candle lights (wax candles should never be lit) illuminate the customary tree decorations, which include flower-filled Julekurv *(woven hearts), colorful woven stars, sheaves of wheat, and friendly* Julenisser *(elves). The fragrant gingerbread hearts, together with the freshness of the Norwegian spruce, produce the time-honored smells of a Scandinavian Christmas.*

FLAG GARLAND

While most households would use only the flags from one country on their garland, we have chosen to include the flags from Norway, Sweden, and Denmark to give a more general Scandinavian flavor.

Materials

The amount of felt and ribbon is enough for a length of garland 20 inches long. Measure the height of your tree to determine how many lengths you need, and the amount of materials required.

Scissors
76 inches white satin ribbon, $\frac{1}{4}$ inch-wide
Bright red felt, 3 x $5\frac{1}{2}$ inches
Tape measure
Medium blue felt, 3 x $2\frac{3}{4}$ inches
9 inches navy blue satin ribbon, $\frac{1}{8}$ inch-wide
28 inches yellow satin ribbon, $\frac{1}{4}$-inch wide
20 inches red satin ribbon, $\frac{1}{4}$-inch wide
Glue

1 Cut six strips of white ribbon, long enough to run from the top to the bottom of the tree.

2 For every 20 inches of white ribbon, cut four red and two blue rectangles of felt, each measuring $2\frac{3}{4}$ x $1\frac{1}{2}$ inches. These will make six flags, two from each country.

3 Referring to the diagrams below, make the following Scandinavian flags:

Norwegian Taking a red felt rectangle, glue a $2\frac{3}{4}$-inch strip of white ribbon along the center of the length of the rectangle. Glue a $1\frac{1}{2}$-inch strip of white ribbon along the center of the width of the rectangle. Glue a strip of navy ribbon along the center of the length and width of the white ribbon already in place.

Danish Taking a red felt rectangle, glue a $2\frac{3}{4}$-inch strip of white ribbon along the center of the length of the rectangle. Glue a $1\frac{1}{2}$-inch strip of white ribbon along the center of the width of the rectangle.

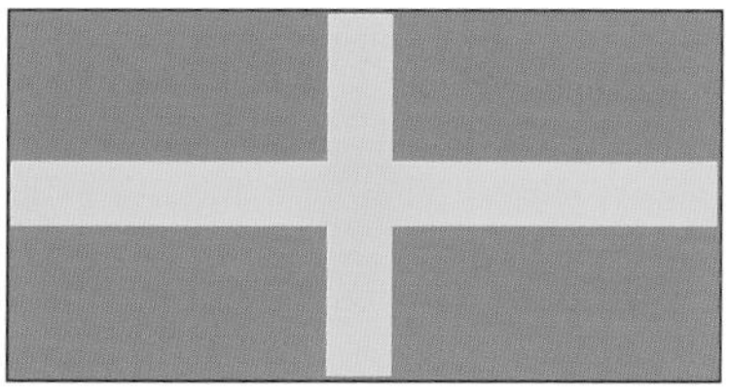

Swedish Taking a medium blue felt rectangle, glue a 2 ¾-inch strip of yellow ribbon along the center of the length of the rectangle. Glue a 1½-inch strip of yellow ribbon along the center of the width of the rectangle.

4 For each 20 inches of the garland, cut two 8-inch lengths each of yellow, red, and white ribbon. Tie them in bows, measuring 1½–2 inches across the loops.

5 Glue on one yellow bow at the top end of the long white ribbon strip. Glue a Danish flag ¾ inch down from the yellow bow. Glue a white bow ¾ inch from the bottom of the flag. Glue a Norwegian flag ¾ inch down from the white bow. Glue a red bow ¾ inch from the bottom of the flag. Glue a Swedish flag ¾ inch down from the red bow. Repeat the pattern to the end of the strip of white ribbon. Repeat with the remaining strips of white ribbon.

6 Wedge all the ribbon bows between the tree branches.

JULENISSER

These small characters are the Scandinavian's version of Santa's helpers (or elves). It was the practice in olden days to put a bowl of *Grøt* (a rice pudding) out in the barn on Christmas Eve. Of course, to this day, one can never be sure who exactly eats the *Grøt*—the *Julenisser* or the neighborhood boys!

MATERIALS

Scissors
Cardboard
Tape measure
Bright red 4-ply yarn (3½ ounces makes 14 *nisser*)
Flesh-colored felt, 3½ x 1½ inches
Red felt, 4⅜ x 4¾ inches per *nisser*
Needle and thread
Glue
Cotton balls
Pair of ⅛-inch eyes
White satin ribbon, ¼ inch wide (approximately 40 inches per *nisser*; 8 inches per bow)
Small gold bell

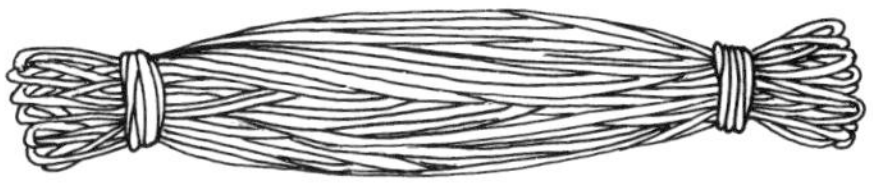

1 Cut two pieces of cardboard, each measuring 6 x 4 inches. Wrap red yarn around the length of one piece of cardboard 20 times (to form 20 loops). Tie off the yarn ¾ inch from each end. This will form the arms.

2 To make the body, wrap red yarn around the second piece of cardboard to form 40 loops.

3 Tie red yarn around all 40 loops of yarn, 3¼ inches from one end and 2¾ inches from the other end. Divide the 3¼-inch length in half to form the legs. Tie red yarn around each leg, ¾ inch from the end.

4 Thread the arms through the yarn loops at the other end, bringing them down to the thread around the top of the legs. Tie red yarn around the body, 1½ inches from the other end of the yarn loops.

5 Glue the flesh-colored felt around the head section of the yarn loops.

6 Cut out two triangular pieces of red felt, and sew the sides together to make the hat. Glue this on the felt head.

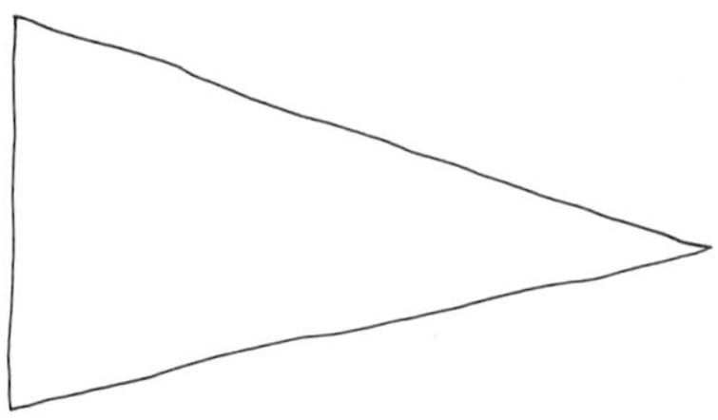

7 Gently shape a cotton ball to form hair and a beard. Glue these into position on the head. Glue the eyes to the face.

8 Glue small white bows on the tied-off sections of the arms and legs, and sew a small gold bell to the top of the hat. Make a hanging loop from white ribbon, and glue or stitch the ends to the hat.

WOVEN STARS

Materials

The instructions given are for the smaller star.
Adjust the measurements to make larger variations.

Scissors
Red and white florist's ribbon, ⅝ inch wide
Needle and clear thread
Invisible-ink marking pen

1 Cut four strips of ribbon 18½ inches long. Fold each strip in half and cut the ends at a 45° angle. Using an invisible-ink pen, mark one end of each strip with a number (1–4) and the other end with that number and letter "a."

2 Carefully refer to the diagrams shown below. With the "a" sides facing away from you, hang strip 2 over the folded strip 1.

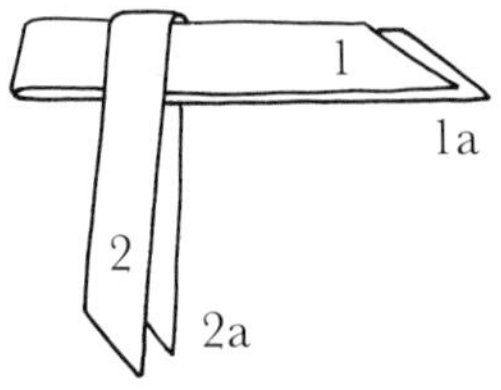

3 Turn the strips counterclockwise so the loop of strip 1 is pointing toward you. Now hang strip 3 over the double strip 2.

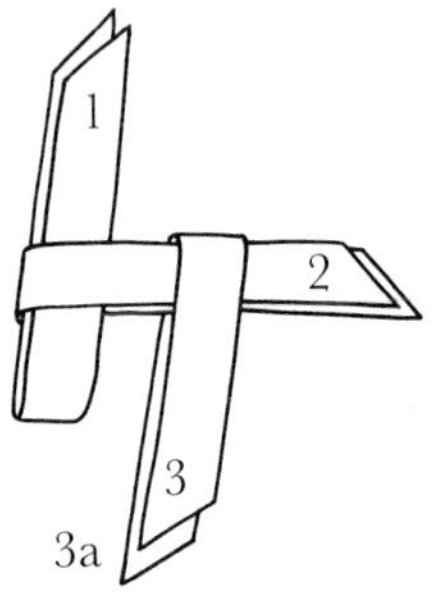

4 Turn the strips counterclockwise again and hang strip 4 over the folded strip 3. Thread the ends through the folded end of strip 1 to form a square.

5 Carefully pull the strips together to close and neaten the square.

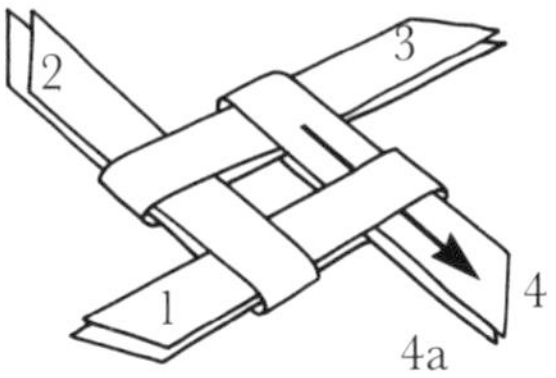

6 Fold strip 4 back across the center to lie beside strips 2 and 2a. Repeat with strips 3, then strip 2, then strip 1. Tuck strip 1 underneath strip 4 to secure it in position, and pull firmly.

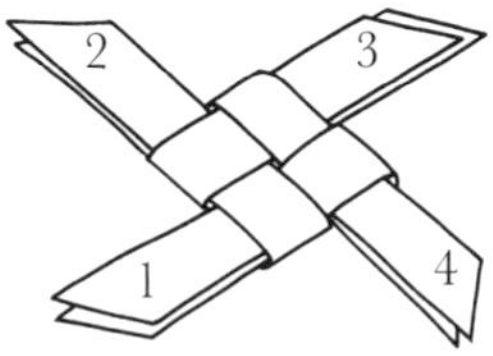

7 Fold strip 1 under and at right angles to lie next to strip 4a. Fold it at right angles again to lie beside strip 1a, across strips 4a and 2.

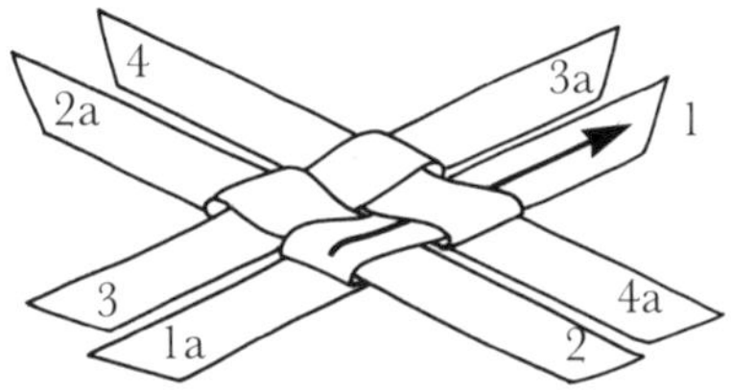

8 Fold this strip back on itself toward the center so triangle B lies on top of triangle A. Tuck the end through the fold underneath. Repeat with strips 2, 3, and 4. Turn the star over and repeat with strips 1a, 2a, 3a, and 4a.

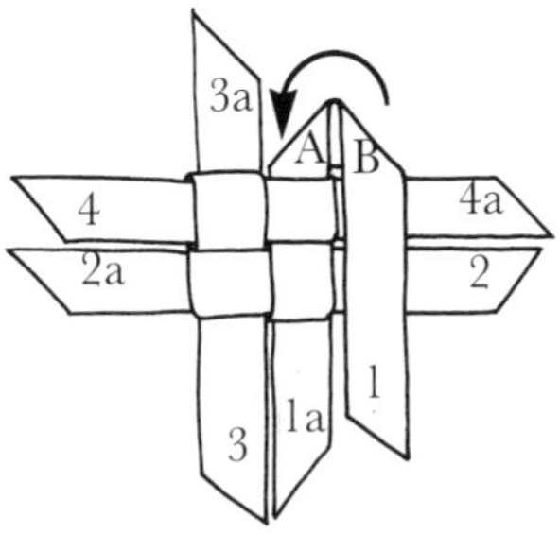

Sheaves of wheat and woven stars

9 Turn the star back to the other side. Bend, but do not fold or crease, strip 1 under itself at right angles until it lies over strip 2a. Hold strip 4 to the side, and bend strip 1 over itself toward the center and slip it under strip 4 to lie over strip 4a. Pull it firmly to make a cone shape. Repeat with strip 2, until it lies over strip 1a. Repeat with strips 3 and 4.

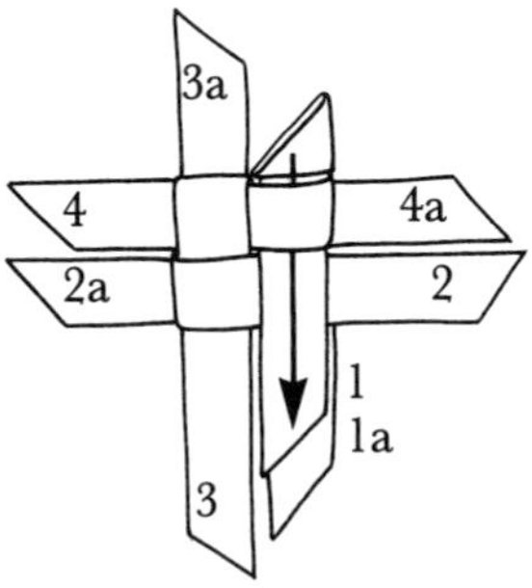

10 Turn the star over and repeat with strips 1a, 2a, 3a, and 4a. Snip off any long ends so they lie evenly with the star shape.

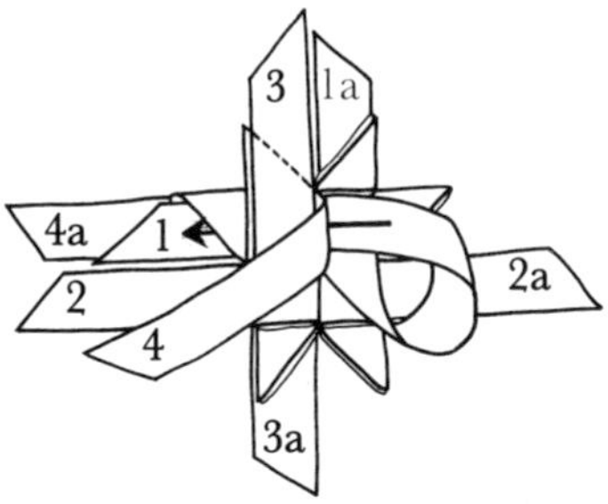

11 Thread the needle with clear thread and stitch a hanging loop at one corner of the star.

SHEAVES OF WHEAT

One of the oldest Scandinavian traditions still practiced today is the fastening of a sheaf of oats to any structure in the garden for the enjoyment of the birds. Not only does this provide the birds with a welcome treat among the tons of snow, but it also offers hours of pleasure for bird-watchers! In this variation on the traditional decoration, I have used wheat instead of oats.

MATERIALS

(per sheaf)

7 stalks of wheat, 8 inches long
Florist's wire
12 inches red satin ribbon, $\frac{1}{4}$ inch wide
Glue

1 Arrange the wheat stalks so they form a triangular shape, with the central sheaf standing upright, and three stalks leaning toward it on the right and left sides.

2 Wire the seven stalks together just at the base of the grain. Leave 2 inches of wire free to attach the sheaf to the tree.

3 Tie a bow with the red satin ribbon. Glue the bow over the wire at the front of the wheat sheaf.

TREETOP WREATH

MATERIALS

The amount of ribbon you need will depend on the distance the wreath must hang from the ceiling to the top of the tree. Adjust to suit your individual measurements.

Tape measure
Straw wreath
Scissors
$4\frac{1}{2}$ yards red satin ribbon, $\frac{5}{8}$ inch wide
Felt-tip pen
Glue
Red thread
Large straw angel
4 small straw angels
4 straw stars

1 Measure the distance the wreath will hang from the ceiling. Double this measurement. Measure around the thickness of the straw wreath. Double this measurement and add to the previous measurement. Cut two lengths of ribbon this length.

2 Using a felt-tip pen, mark the straw wreath into quarters. Take the cut end of one long strip of ribbon and wrap it around one mark on the wreath. Take the other cut end of the same ribbon strip and wrap it around the mark at the opposite side of the wreath. Glue the ribbon ends to secure. Repeat with the other long piece of ribbon around the remaining felt-tip marks on the wreath.

Treetop wreath

3 Tie four ribbon bows and glue these over the seam where the ribbon strips wrap around the straw wreath.

4 Take a 20-inch length of ribbon and tie a bow around the two loops, about 2 inches from the top.

5 Tie red thread to the angels and stars. Hang the large angel from the bow at the top center so it dangles a little way below the middle of the straw wreath. Position the stars to hang from the ribbon surrounding the straw wreath. Place the small angels to hang below the straw wreath, centrally between the straw stars.

WOVEN BASKET

Traditionally made from red and white paper or felt, these charming heart-shaped woven baskets, or *Julekurv*, usually hold candy when hung on the Christmas tree. For a light, feathery effect, I have filled this *Julekurv* with small bunches of baby's breath, instead of the traditional candies. On the festive Scandinavian table (see page 82), these woven baskets also serve as napkin holders, each with a little treat hidden at the bottom.

MATERIALS

White felt, $9\frac{1}{2}$ x 3 inches
Red felt, $9\frac{1}{2}$ x 3 inches
Glue
Red felt, $9\frac{1}{2}$ x $\frac{3}{4}$ inches
Flowers or candy to fill the basket

1 Fold the piece of white felt in half and cut it according to the pattern given on page 123. Repeat with the larger piece of red felt.

2 Weave the felt strips, as illustrated opposite to make the basket.

3 Glue the narrow strip of red felt to opposite sides of the inside center of the top of the woven heart. Fill it with flowers or candy, as wished.

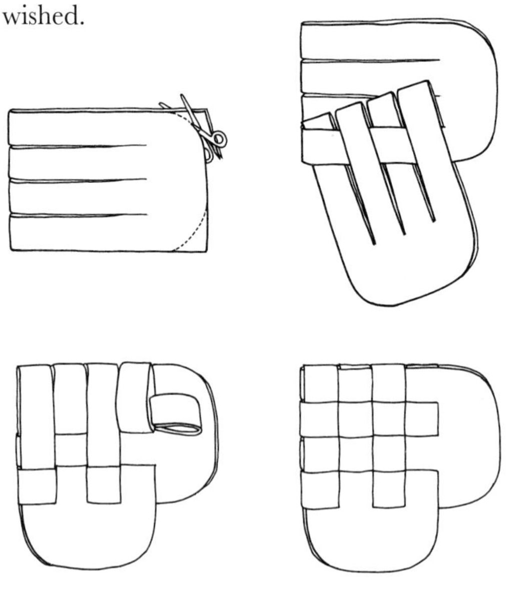

PEPPERKAKER

GINGERBREAD COOKIES

According to tradition, to be a good Scandinavian housewife you must make seven varieties of Christmas cookies. *Pepperkaker* is just one of these cookies. Made with ground ginger, and black pepper for that special "kick," it is a delicious snack. It is often used to make gingerbread houses and ornaments.

MATERIALS

$\frac{1}{4}$ cup light corn syrup
3 teaspoons cinnamon
$\frac{1}{2}$ teaspoon black pepper
2 teaspoons ground cloves
$1\frac{1}{2}$ teaspoons ground ginger
Small saucepan
Wooden spoon
1 cup softened butter
$\frac{3}{4}$ cup sugar
Mixing bowl
1 egg

Gingerbread cookies

3 $^1/_2$ cups all-purpose flour
1 $^1/_2$ teaspoons baking soda
Rolling pin
Heart cookie cutters
Skewer or toothpick
Baking sheet
Wire rack

Frosting:
1 egg white
1–2 teaspoons white vinegar
Confectioner's sugar
Food coloring (optional)
Knife or metal spatula
Lengths of ribbon for hangers

1 Heat the syrup and spices in a small saucepan, stirring until the mixture begins to boil. Remove from the heat and let cool.

2 Cream the butter and sugar in a mixing bowl. Stir in the syrup mixture and the egg.

3 Slowly stir in the flour and baking soda. Mix to a smooth dough. Cover and refrigerate overnight.

4 Roll out the dough to a thickness of $^1/_8$–$^1/_4$ inch. Using heart-shaped cookie cutters, cut the dough into hearts of varying sizes. Make a small hole at the top of each heart with a skewer or toothpick (for threading the hanger through later).

5 Bake on a floured baking sheet at 400°F for 5 to 8 minutes. Remove to a wire rack and allow to cool.

6 When the cookies have cooled, make the frosting by mixing together the egg white and vinegar. Add confectioner's sugar until you achieve the consistency of custard. Add food coloring, if using. Carefully spread the frosting on the cookies with a knife or spatula. Let harden.

7 Thread a ribbon through the hole at the top of each heart to make a hanging loop, knot the ends securely, and hang the *pepperkaker* from the tree.

Table Setting

In Scandinavia, the festivities begin on Christmas Eve. In Norway, the day starts with a special raisin bread eaten in the morning, while the father puts a sheaf of oats outside the kitchen window for the birds. After a simple lunch, younger Scandinavian children are sent to bed, while the older ones go skiing. During this time, the parents decorate the tree. The children wake to ringing church bells and the magical tree in the late afternoon, when the family gather together to read the Christmas story and say a blessing for the feast that follows, which includes such traditional dishes as Rømmegrøt, *a sour cream porridge, and seven different types of cookie.*

This Scandinavian table is draped with gorgeous hand-embroidered linen, using a traditional Christmas theme. Greenery and candles surround the crowning Kransekake, *or garland cake, of our Scandinavian table, decorated in customary style with miniature flags.* Julekurv *placed on the dinner plates hold the napkins, in addition to a tiny gift, which pops out as the napkin is removed.*

WREATH CAKE

This is a traditional cake used at all special occasions in Scandinavia, such as at Christmas, weddings, and anniversaries.

Materials

3 cups almonds
Saucepan
Water
Food processor
$2\frac{1}{2}$ cups confectioner's sugar
2 egg whites
Aluminum foil
About 2 cups marzipan
Rolling pin
Pencil
Baking parchment
Ruler

Glaze:

1 egg white
$1\frac{1}{3}$ cups confectioner's sugar
2-3 drops clear vinegar
Pastry bag and writing tips
Miniature flags and crackers for decoration

1 Plunge half of the almonds into boiling water for 30 seconds to loosen the skins and blanch them.

2 Place all the almonds in a food processor and grind coarsely. Add the confectioner's sugar to the processor and grind the mixture to a fine consistency.

3 Add the egg whites and mix for 30 seconds at a medium speed, then another 30 seconds at the highest speed. The mixture should form a dough.

4 Wrap the dough in a piece of aluminum foil and place in a cold oven. Set the oven at 200°F. Leave the dough in the oven for about 1 hour.

5 Leave the dough to cool to body temperature. Gradually work the marzipan into the dough with your hands. Roll the dough into "snake" shapes of a finger thickness.

6 Draw out 16 circles on the baking parchment. The smallest circle should be $1\frac{1}{2}$ inches in diameter. Each circle should be increased by $\frac{1}{2}$ inch, up to the largest, which will be $7\frac{1}{2}$ inches in diameter. (Alternatively, special baking pans can be purchased from Scandinavian specialty stores.)

7 Bake at 400°F for 8 to 10 minutes. Cool the rings quickly. The rings can be frozen or stored in an airtight container with a piece of bread (to prevent them from drying out). Place sufficient "snake" shapes of dough around the edge of each parchment circle to form a ring.

8 Mix up the glaze to a runny consistency. Place the largest ring on a plate. Using the pastry bag fitted with a writing tip, pipe the glaze onto the ring in a zigzag pattern, starting at the top of the ring. Place the next size of ring on top; the glaze will anchor it. Repeat with each successively smaller ring to form a tower.

9 Decorate the wreath cake with miniature flags and Christmas favors. When cutting the cake to eat it, remove and cut the largest ring first to maintain the tower shape.

Opposite *Despite the long cold winter days and nights, Scandinavian homes reflect a cozy atmosphere with the introduction of rich, bright reds to warm the stark white and natural tones they favor. This inviting window sends a warm welcome to family and friends, as well as passing strangers, with its display of woven stars and dangling night-lights, and profuse array of glowing candles.*

CHAPTER 6

A Victorian Theme

IT WAS DURING THE LAST CENTURY that the festive custom of decorating an evergreen tree inside the home was introduced. The Victorians had very little money to spend on extravagant decorations, yet they were enthusiastic in their celebration of the Christmas season, adapting customs from other eras and countries.

The Victorian middle classes placed great emphasis on the family. Family members spent a lot of time designing and creating personal gifts for each other, a tradition that even extended to special household servants. They spent long, happy hours together, planning and creating decorations for the tree and home. Their love of laces, satins, ribbons, and exotic flourishes were reflected in this preparation for what became a very special season.

Many typical Victorian decorations for the tree, table, and the home, are featured in this chapter, enabling you to re-create your own Victorian Christmas.

Tree Decorations

In Victorian times, small lit candles would have made the tree glow at night. These days, for safety reasons, we use miniature electric lights in the shape of small white candles to light an evergreen tree, enhancing its lush and glistening array of decorations.

TREE SKIRT

MATERIALS

Scissors
$1^3/_4$ yards velvet fabric, 44 inches wide
$2^1/_4$ yards lace-covered satin fabric, 44 nches wide
14 yards insertion cord
Needle and thread
12-inch ruler

1 To make segment pattern, place a 25-inch paper square down flat. Measure from the bottom left corner, along the bottom edge, and mark at 5 inches. Repeat from the bottom left corner, going up the left edge.

2 To mark curve, tie a pencil to one end of a 30-inch length of string. Take loose ends of string in one hand and pencil in the other. Place string along bottom edge of paper. Put pencil on the 5-inch mark, and trap loose end of string under your thumb, keeping it taut over the bottom left corner. You can check first by swinging the string in an arc across the paper, to make sure the pencil will pass through both marks. When satisfied, mark out the arc. Repeat this process for the 25-inch mark (the arc will cross from bottom right to top left corners). Cut out along the two arcs. Fold pattern in half and cut along folded edge. Use segment patterns to cut four velvet and four satin pieces allowing $^1/_4$ inch larger for seam allowances.

3 With right sides together, cut one pattern piece each of velvet and lace-covered satin. Insert insertion cord and sew along the edge, leaving a $^1/_4$-inch seam allowance.

4 Join the remaining six sections in the same way, alternating between satin and velvet, and making sure the cord is inserted between each section. Do *not* sew up the last seam to make a continuous circle; instead, leave a gap. Sew cord along one side of the gap only. Baste the cord to the right side around the outside edge.

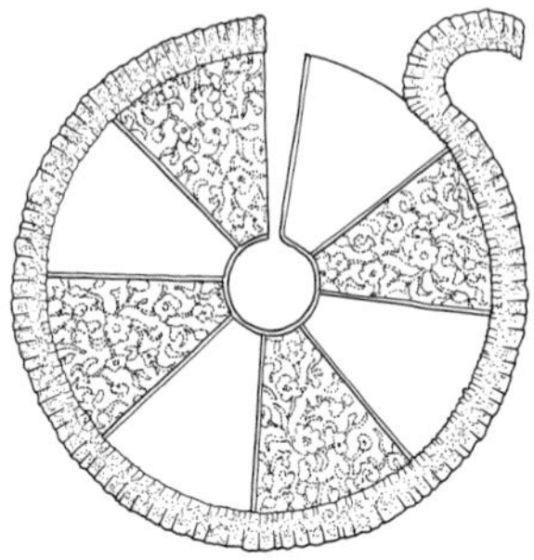

5 Take a strip of lace-covered satin, 5 inches wide and about 16 feet long. Turn under one long edge about $^1/_4$ inch and hem. Run a gathering stitch along the other long edge. Pull up the gathers and attach the fabric to the outside edge of the skirt, with right sides together, under the insertion cord.

6 Finally, stitch under the top edge of tree skirt and press.

BASKET ANGEL

MATERIALS

Wicker angel shape
Gold spray-paint
Needle and thread
Cream or ivory lace—the amount depends on the size of the wicker angel used. For this angel, we used:
24 inches flat lace, 4 inches wide
15 inches gathered lace, ½ inch wide
10 inches flat or gathered lace, 1 inch wide
Low-temperature glue gun and glue sticks
30 inches fused pearl strand
30 inches gold cord
Ribbon roses
Ribbon

1 In a well-ventilated area, spray the wicker angel shape with two coats of gold paint.

2 Run two lines of gathering stitches along the top edge of the wide flat lace. Pull the stitches up to gather the lace. Place it around the wicker angel, just under the wings. Tie the threads at the back to form a high-waisted skirt. Secure the gathered edge to the wicker angel with hot glue.

3 Glue the ½-inch wide gathered lace to the back of the wings, along the outside edge. Glue the pearl strand and gold cord over the lace heading that has just been glued to the back of the wings. Glue pearls and gold cord to the front of the wings, along the edge of where the lace emerges.

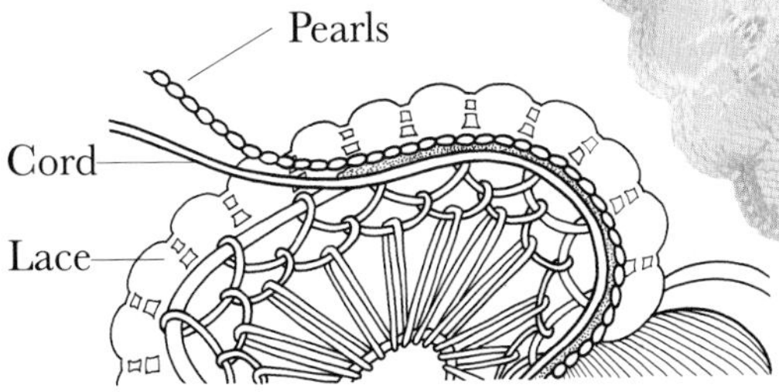

4 Take the 1-inch wide lace and cut it into two pieces, one for each sleeve. Stitch a row of gathering stitches along the inside edge and pull it tight to form a circle. Shape this circle into a sleeve by flattening it into a cone shape. Glue the gathered edge to the wicker arms, just above the top edge of the lace skirt.

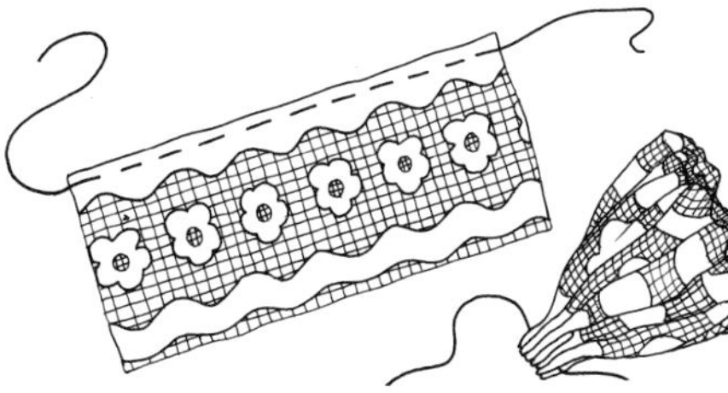

5 Glue a posy of ribbon roses behind and around the hands. This will look like the angel is carrying a bouquet, while at the same time covering the skirt and sleeve lace edges. Tie a ribbon bow with long tails and glue it to the bottom of the posy.

VICTORIAN FAN

Materials

1 yard fine wire braid
12 inches stiff flat lace, 3–3½ inches wide
Low-temperature glue gun and glue sticks
Florist's wire
1 small tassel
8 inches thin gold cord
Hair spray
Ultra-fine gold glitter
1 yard burgundy satin ribbon, ⅛ inch wide
Baby's breath
1 ribbon rosebud

1 Thread 12 inches of the wire braid through the top edge of the stiff flat lace. Fold the lace accordion-style, and pinch it together at the bottom edge. Glue the cut edges of the lace down, and wrap florist's wire around the bottom edge to secure.

2 Glue or wire the tassel to the bottom edge. Thread a 5-inch piece of thin gold cord through the lace in the center top of the fan. Form a loop by knotting the two ends.

3 Spray the lace lightly with hair spray. While still damp, sprinkle it very lightly with ultra-fine gold glitter. Spray again lightly to set. Let the lace dry completely before shaking off the excess glitter.

4 Make a triple loop bow, 3 inches wide, from the burgundy ribbon, and wrap florist's wire around the center to secure. Make a triple loop bow, 2 inches wide, from the remaining fine wire braid.

5 Glue the burgundy ribbon bow over the wired bottom edge of the fan. Glue a small amount of baby's breath over the ribbon bow. Next glue the fine wire braid bow over the baby's breath, and finish by gluing the ribbon rosebud in the center of the gold bow.

CORNUCOPIA

Materials

Decorative wrapping paper,
5 x 10 inches
Glue
Tracing paper
Pencil
Scissors
Low-temperature glue gun and glue sticks
12 inches heavy wire gold cord
1 yard white satin ribbon, ⅛ inch wide
Florist's wire
12 inches gold grosgrain ribbon, ⅛ inch wide
1 ribbon rose bow
Needle
12 inches thin gold cord
Baby's breath
3 dried burgundy-colored rosebuds

1 Fold the wrapping paper in half to form a 5-inch square with the decorated side facing outward. Glue the underside of the paper and seal the square closed. Let to dry.

2 Trace the cornucopia pattern (page 123) onto one side of the square; cut it out. Roll it into a cone shape, overlapping the paper slightly at the front, and secure with glue.

3 Starting at the top of the cone, at the front where the seam is, glue a length of heavy wire gold cord around the top edge. Glue another piece of cord over the seam, placing the edge of the cord at the top of the cone and running it down, 2 inches past the bottom point.

4 Wrap a small piece of ribbon around the bottom point of the cord and paper cone to secure. Unravel the 2 inches of cord hanging below the point to create a tassel effect.

Opposite *Victorian fan and cornucopia*

5 Make a triple loop bow with the white satin ribbon, leaving 3-inch long tails. Using florist's wire, wire the bow in the center to secure, and glue to the top front of the cone. Form a single loop collar bow from the gold ribbon and glue it over the white bow. Glue a white ribbon rose bow over the top.

6 Use a needle to thread the length of thin gold cord through the paper at the back of the cone. Tie the two ends together to form a loop.

7 Fill the paper cone with the baby's breath and small dried rosebuds.

HOBBY HORSE

Materials

Tracing paper
Pencil
Burgundy satin, 5 x 10 inches
Flat lace, 5 x 10 inches
Scissors
Needle and thread
7–8 inches ribbon, 1/8 inch wide
5-inch wooden dowel, painted gold, 1/4 inch thick
Glue
Batting or toy stuffing
2 faceted beads, 4mm
Strong thread
14 inches gathered lace, 1 inch wide
14 inches cream fused pearl strand
20 inches gold cord
Ribbon, ribbon roses, and beads for decoration

1 Trace the hobby horse head and ear patterns (see page 122). Position the tracing over the fabric to cut out two pieces of satin and two pieces of flat lace for the head, and two pieces of each for the ears.

2 Place the lace over the right side of the satin and sew the head pieces together (right side of lace-topped fabric together), leaving an opening at the bottom.

3 Wrap the ribbon spirally around the wooden dowel. Secure at each end with a dab of glue.

4 Turn the head right sides out and stuff it lightly with batting. Place the dowel into the center of the neck opening and continue stuffing around the dowel. Hand-stitch the bottom of the neck to secure.

5 Place the lace ear over the satin ear and glue them together to prevent the satin from fraying. Fold one ear in half lengthwise and oversew the bottom edge. Repeat with the other ear. Stitch the ears into place on either side of the head.

6 Stitch the beads to the head to form eyes. Use strong thread to pull the beads in tightly, forming small indentations.

7 Starting from between the ears, hand-stitch or glue the gathered lace down the outside seam of the head to create the mane. Glue or stitch the pearl strand along the edge of the lace, where it attaches to the head.

8 Place gold cord around the nose and around the head to form the halter. Attach cord reins to the cord halter.

9 Decorate the hobby horse with ribbon, ribbon roses, and beads. Have fun creating your own design.

PARASOL

Materials

5-inch wooden dowel, 1/4 inch wide
Gold acrylic paint
Paintbrush
8 inches burgundy ribbon, 1/8 inch wide
Glue or low-temperature glue gun and glue sticks
Scissors
Ivory or cream net, 6 inches square
Burgundy moiré fabric, 6 inches square
24 inches ivory or cream lace, 1/2 inch wide
Tissue paper
Florist's wire
9 inches burgundy ribbon, 1/4 inch wide
5 inches burgundy ribbon, 1/16 inch wide

1 Paint the wooden dowel with gold paint and let dry. Paint a second coat, if one is necessary. Wrap 1/8-inch wide ribbon spirally

Hobby horse and parasol

around the dowel. Finally, secure the ribbon ends with small dabs of glue.

2 At one end of the dowel, form a small ribbon loop. Cover the ends of the loop with a piece of ribbon wrapped around the end of the wooden dowel.

3 Cut a $5\frac{1}{2}$-inch circle out of both the net and the moiré fabric. Glue lace around the outside edge of the net only.

4 To find the exact center of the moiré fabric circle, fold it in half, then into quarters. Crease the folds slightly to mark the center point. Lay the net circle on a work surface with the wrong side facing up. Lay the moiré fabric directly over the net with the wrong side facing up.

5 Dab some glue at the center point of the moiré fabric, and place the bottom end of the dowel (without a ribbon loop) over that point, so the dowel is vertical. Mold some tissue paper around the bottom half of the dowel.

6 Bring the fabric and net over the tissue and secure with wire, $\frac{1}{2}$ inch below the glued-on lace ruffle. Trim away any excess wire.

7 Wrap the wider ribbon around the tip of the dowel (step 5) and over the wire (step 6). Form a loop from the narrower ribbon and glue to the front of the parasol. Top with a bow made from the remaining ribbon.

Padded angel and button wreath

PADDED ANGEL

MATERIALS

Decorative felt, 6 x 12 inches
$^1/_2$ round shoulder pad, or cut pattern (see page 123) from foam, $^1/_4$ inch thick
Fabric glue
Scissors
1 large wooden bead with a large hole in one side
Acrylic paint
Small paintbrush
Pinking shears (optional)
Large needle and strong carpet thread
12 inches gold metallic rickrack
1 large gold star
Low temperature glue gun and glue sticks
1 small gold star
5 inches gold cord
Small piece of a gold-colored, coiled scouring pad
10 inches gold-edged, white satin ribbon, $^1/_8$ inch wide
1 tiny gold rosebud
10 inches gold mesh wire ribbon, $1^1/_2$ inches wide
Cloth-covered wire

1 Fold the piece of decorative felt in half, enclosing the shoulder pad or foam shape inside, with the straight edge of the shoulder pad against the fold. Apply a liberal amount of fabric glue around the curved edge of the shoulder pad and press the felt down firmly with your fingers to close. Run a thumbnail or closed scissors tip around the edge to make sure that the glue bonds well. Leave the glue to dry for 4 to 6 hours.

2 Using a small paintbrush, paint the large wooden bead with a coat of flesh-colored acrylic paint. Paint on the eyes using the round handle end of a paintbrush to form two dots. Paint two round circles for the cheeks.

3 Cut around the curved edge of the pad, through the glued portion, to trim the excess felt (see facing page). It is particularly effective if you use pinking shears.

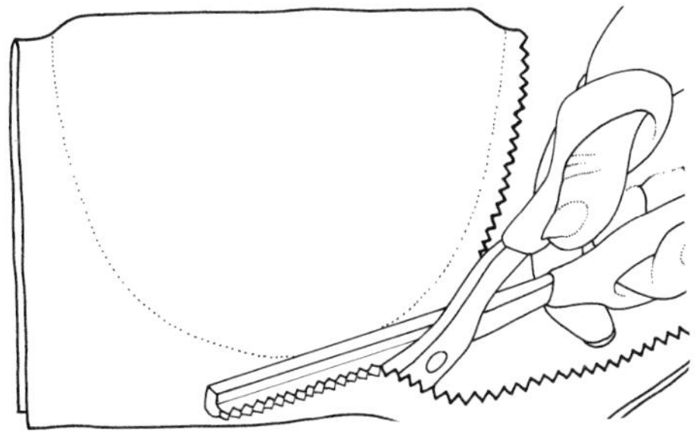

4 Fold the two corners toward the center and overlap them slightly. Using a large, heavy needle and carpet thread, secure the corners down with a few catchstitches, with a knot at the back.

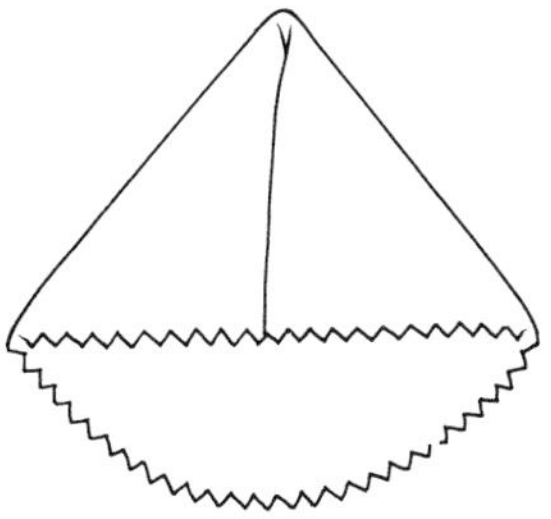

5 Glue the gold rickrack onto the felt, about ½ inch above the cut edge. Start in the front on one side, and run it around the back to end up in front where you started. Cover the seam of the two cut ends by gluing on the large star using the glue gun. Glue the small star over the knot at the back, arranging the trim in an attractive way.

6 Glue the painted head bead on the point at the top. Form a loop from the gold cord and glue it to the top of the head to make a hanging loop. Cover the glued end of the loop with pieces of gold scouring pad for cute hair curls. Trim where necessary.

7 Make a collar bow for the angel with the gold-edged ribbon and glue it under the chin of the head bead. Glue a rosebud to the center of the bow.

8 Form a circle with mesh wire ribbon, overlapping the ends slightly. Wind wire around the middle of the loop to form a bow. Glue to the center of the back of the angel to create wings.

BUTTON WREATH

Materials

Craft knife
Pair of compasses
Heavy gold board or mat
Gold acrylic paint
Small paintbrush
Low-temperature glue gun and glue sticks
Assorted white buttons
Assorted gold buttons
15 inches gold mesh wire ribbon, 1½ inches wide
Small piece of florist's wire
5 inches gold cord

1 Using a craft knife and a pair of compasses, cut a 4-inch circle from the board or mat. Cut a 1¾-inch hole in the center. Paint the outer white edge of the board circle with the gold paint.

2 Glue white buttons to the inner white side of the circle in an attractive way. Glue a few gold buttons in between the white buttons to add some interest.

3 Form a circle with the mesh wire ribbon, overlapping the ends slightly. Wind florist's wire around the middle of the loop to form a bow. Set aside.

4 Form a loop from the gold cord and attach it to the top of the wreath to form the hanging loop. Glue the bow formed in step 3 over the knot of the hanging loop. Cover the wired center of the bow with a small decorative button.

DOILY BASKET

MATERIALS

Crocheted doily (round or heart-shaped),
4 inches wide
Fabric stiffener
Damp sponge
Toothpick
Aluminum foil
Small, round bottle, approximately 1 inch in diameter
4 inches crocheted lace, ½ inch wide
Low-temperature glue gun and glue sticks
24 inches burgundy satin ribbon, $^{1}/_{16}$ inch wide
1 medium folded ribbon rosebud
2 sprigs green moss
Baby's breath

1 Coat the doily on both sides with fabric stiffener, applying it with your fingers. Pat the doily well with the damp sponge to remove the excess stiffener. Use a toothpick to poke through the holes in the doily to clear them of the stiffener.

2 Wrap aluminum foil around a small round bottle. Wrap the doily around the bottle and let dry overnight.

3 Apply fabric stiffener to the crocheted lace with your fingers, as in step 1. Allow the lace to dry flat.

4 To assemble the basket, glue each end of the flat lace to opposite sides of the doily basket base.

5 Make a $2^{1}/_{2}$ inch triple loop bow from the burgundy ribbon. Glue it to one side of the basket, where the handle and basket meet. Glue a ribbon rosebud to the center of the bow.

6 Fill the basket with green moss and scatter baby's breath over the top for extra interest.

DOILY HEART

MATERIALS

Papier-mâché heart, 3 inches wide
Gold metallic acrylic paint
Paintbrush
Crocheted doily, 6 inches in diameter
Cloth-covered wire
24 inches burgundy satin ribbon, $^{1}/_{16}$ inch wide
Low-temperature glue gun and glue sticks
1 ribbon rose
Gold hanging cord (if necessary)

1 Paint the papier-mâché heart with a coat of gold metallic acrylic paint and leave to dry.

2 Place the heart in the center of the doily and gather up the edges of the doily neatly (see the diagram). Check to make sure the heart is centered, and secure the doily edges by wrapping around with wire.

3 Arrange the gathers evenly to form a small lace circle. Lay the gathers back against the heart. Make a 2-inch wide bow from the burgundy ribbon and glue it just above the gathers. Glue a ribbon rose in the center of the gathers.

4 If the papier-mâché heart does not have a hanger attached, make one from a loop of gold cord. Pull the hanger through a gap in the doily at the top of the heart.

Opposite *Doily basket and doily heart*

PRESENT ORNAMENTS

MATERIALS

Cardboard or poster board
Pencil
Ruler
Scissors
Glue
Decorative wrapping paper
Florist's ribbon, 2 inches wide
Cord

1 Using the pattern given on page 124, draw out the box shapes on cardboard with a pencil and ruler. Cut out the box shapes. Score along the foldlines using a pair of scissors to make neater folds, and glue the small tabs to construct the box.

2 For each box, cut out one piece of wrapping paper measuring 6 x 3 inches.

3 Starting in the center of one side panel of the box, wrap the length of the paper around it until it slightly overlaps the other cut edge of the paper (this should be in the center of the side panel, which can then be covered by ribbon). Glue the paper down to secure. When dry, fold the ends of the paper down like an envelope. Glue to secure. Repeat with the other side.

4 Cut the ribbon into the following lengths: one piece 22 inches long; one piece 8 inches long. Tear each of these into eight strips (making each strip 1/4 inch wide). For each box, you will need one strip measuring 22 inches long and 1/4 inch wide, and eight strips measuring 8 inches long and 1/4 inch wide.

5 Wrap the longer strip of ribbon around the box. Start by leaving a 3–4 inch tail. After wrapping it around once and returning to the beginning, twist the ribbon and wrap it around the other side. Take the remaining loose end of ribbon, wrap it under the twist of ribbon at the top, and pull it through. Pull it taut and tie once, if you wish.

6 Tie the shorter strips of ribbon tightly onto the top of the box. Curl the ribbon strips by holding one strip at a time, as close to the central knot as possible, between the thumb and sharp edge of the scissors. Pull firmly to the end to form a curl. Repeat, holding more tightly if a tighter curl is preferred. Curl the ends of ribbon that formed the knot.

7 Cut a 10 inch length of cord. Carefully slip one cut end under the central knot holding the curls. Pull through to the other side. Tie the two ends of the cord in a tight reef knot. Trim the ends, if necessary, and gently pull the loop around so the knot slides under the central ribbon knot, hidden under the ribbon curls.

Gift ornaments (page 97) and miniature favors

MINIATURE FAVORS

MATERIALS

Colored foil paper, $6\frac{1}{2}$ x 4 inches
Cardboard or poster board, 2 x $3\frac{3}{4}$ inches
Glue
2 cylinders (plastic piping, 1 inch in diameter), 6 inches long and 4 inches long
Paper towels
Waxed cord
Florist's ribbon
Scissors

Because these favors are for decorative purposes only, you will not need jokes or toys to stuff inside.

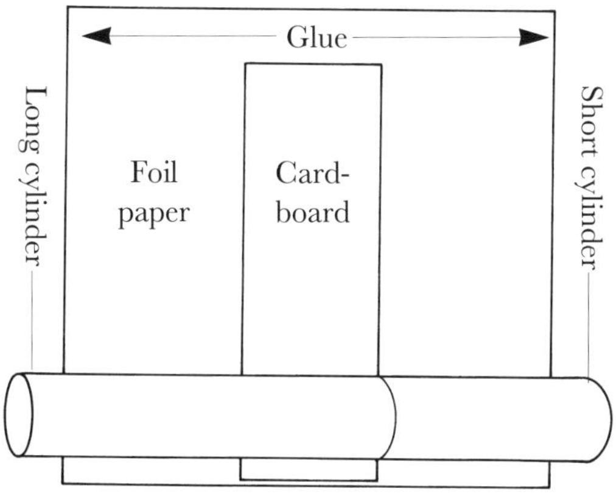

1 Place the foil paper, colored side down, on the work surface. Place the cardboard in the center of the foil, along the bottom edge. Spread glue along the top edge of the foil paper (see the diagram).

2 Place the long cylinder horizontally on the bottom left and the short cylinder horizontally on the bottom right of the foil, butting the ends of the forms along the right-hand edge of the cardboard. Tightly roll the foil around the cylinders, holding the forms together, until you have rolled the foil up to reach the glue.

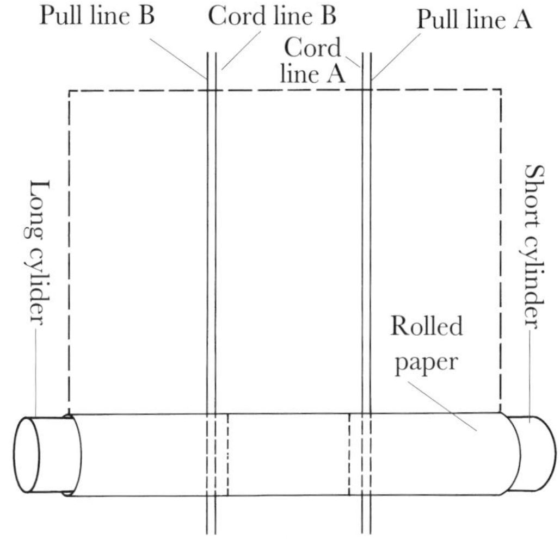

Continue rolling over the glued edge. Wipe away any excess glue with a paper towel, and let dry.

3 Taking the short former on the right, pull it about $\frac{1}{4}$ inch away from the right-hand edge of the cardboard (called "pull line A" on the diagram). Wrap the waxed cord twice around the foil, centrally between the right-hand edge of the cardboard and the left-hand edge of the short cylinder (called "cord line A" on the diagram).

4 Holding the two ends of the waxed cord, pull them in opposite directions. This will cause the cord to form a crease at the edge of the cardboard. Push the short cylinder back against the long cylinder and the cardboard to shape the favor. Remove the waxed cord, then remove the short cylinder.

5 Take the long tube on the left and pull it to "pull line B". Wrap the cord twice around the foil at "cord line B". Pull the cord tightly, as in step 4. To shape the favor, gently push the long cylinder tube back against the card-board. Remove cord and cylinder.

6 Decorate the favor with ribbon, curling it by running a scissor blade along its length, and tying it in the creased sides of the favor.

ICICLES

Materials
(per icicle)

Needle-nosed pliers
4 inches white chenille (12 inches of chenille stem cut into thirds)
Cord or strong thread for hanging
6 crystal sunburst beads (12mm)
6 crystal sunburst beads (10mm)
3 crystal faceted beads (8mm)
3 crystal faceted beads (6mm)
2 crystal faceted beads (4mm)
Glue
Wire cutters or strong scissors
Ribbon rose, ribbon bow, and lace bow for decoration (optional)

1 Using the pliers, form a small tight loop at one end of the chenille. Thread cord or strong thread through the loop and tie in a knot to make a hanging loop.

2 Thread beads onto the chenille in the following order: 6 sunburst beads, 12mm; 6 sunburst beads, 10mm; 3 faceted beads, 8mm; 3 faceted beads, 6mm; 1 faceted bead, 4mm. Push them up to the looped end and twist until they slot together. The fit must be tight; however, if there is any difficulty pushing the beads onto the chenille, trim away some bristles along the wire.

3 Dab glue on the end of the chenille; thread the last 4mm faceted bead. Rotate the bead so the glue spreads around. Wipe away excess glue. Trim any excess chenille with wire cutters or scissors.

4 Decorate the icicle, as wished. Here a ribbon rose has been glued over a satin ribbon bow and lace bow for a Victorian flavor.

WINTER WONDERLAND

Materials

Glue
16 inches gold braided metallic cord, 1/32 inch wide
2 crystal squat bicone beads, 18 x 16mm
2 crystal squat bicone beads, 13 x 10mm
2 crystal elongated bicone beads, 13 x 6mm
2 crystal faceted round beads, 8mm
2 crystal faceted round beads, 10mm
10 gold-washed floral rondelle beads, 6mm
2 gold-washed round beads, 4mm
Scissors
14 inches gold glitter ribbon, 5/8 inch wide

1 Dab glue on both ends of the cord to keep them from unraveling while stringing on the beads. Tie an overhand knot at one end of the cord. String on the beads, as shown.

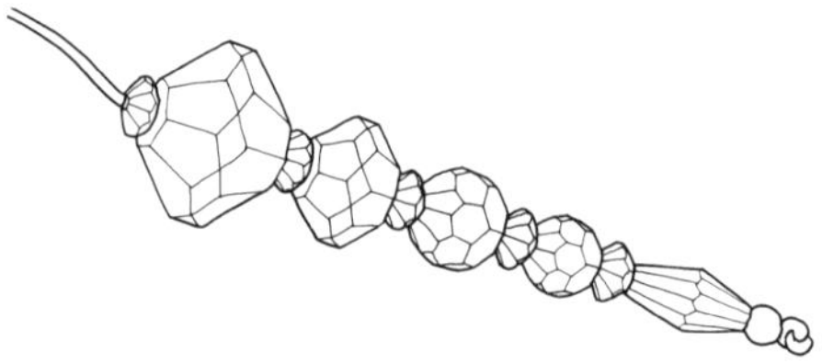

2 String on step 1 beads in reverse order. Tie an overhand knot in the other end of the cord. Dab glue on both knots. When it has dried, trim away the cord ends close to the knots. Slide the two sets of beads to the opposite ends of the cord, as shown.

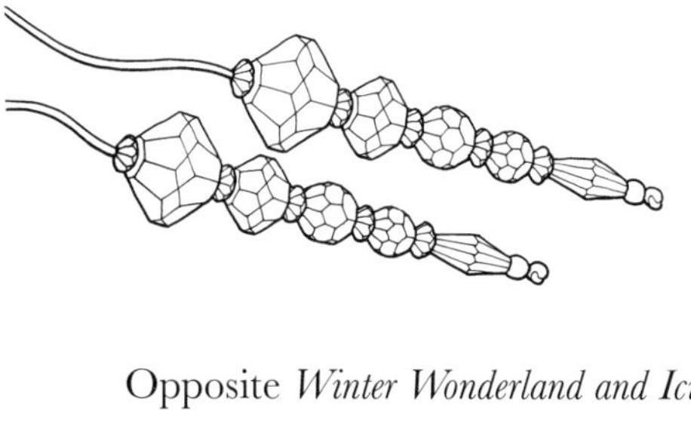

Opposite *Winter Wonderland and Icicles*

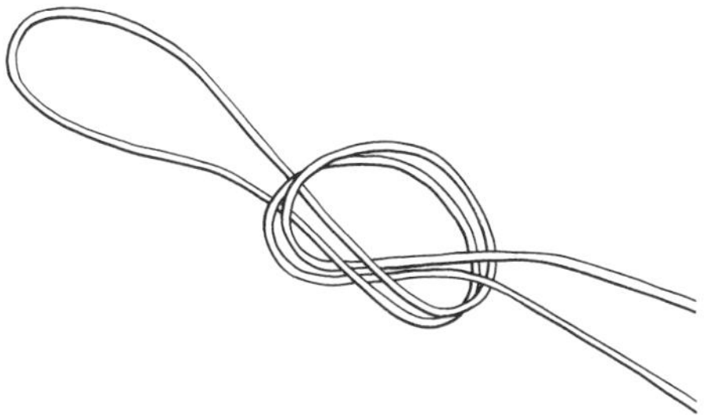

Tying an overhand knot

3 Fold the cord so one icicle is approximately 1 inch lower than the other. Tie an overhand knot 1½ inches from the fold, forming a loop to hang on the tree.

4 Tie a bow with the gold ribbon over the top of the overhand knot.

Table Setting

Victorians were great home lovers, and the Christmas festivities provided them with an opportunity to celebrate with friends and family. Special treats, which were only served once a year or on very rare occasions, were lavishly provided to tempt every palate. To frame this array of culinary delights, the Christmas table setting was made extra special with a rich collection of homemade garlands and decorations.

This table is decorated with a lacy tablecloth. Table runners in rich burgundy provide the background to the table service. The decorative theme is set by the two-tiered centerpiece of golden wicker, greenery, pinecones, and fruit, flanked by the rosy glow of warm candlelight, while napkin rings of ribbon, adorned with a miniature wicker wreath to coordinate with the centerpiece, are decorated with a profusion of satin ribbons, roses, and pearls.

Napkin rings, above (page 105), and table centerpiece, right (page 104)

TABLE CENTERPIECE

MATERIALS

Wicker wreath, 12 inches in diameter
Wicker wreath, 9 inches in diameter
Gold spray-paint
Scissors
5 yards gold-edged wine moiré ribbon, 1 inch wide
Low-temperature glue gun and glue sticks
1 stand for fireplace tools, without the tools
Florist's wire
4 yards gold-edged wine moiré ribbon, $1\frac{1}{2}$ inches wide
Floral sprays for decoration

1 Spray the two wicker wreaths with gold paint in a well-ventilated area. Let dry.

2 Cut four pieces of the narrower ribbon, each 30 inches long. Wrap them, one at a time, and an equal distance apart, around the larger wreath. Tie the ends in a knot. Glue the knot underneath the wreath, out of sight.

3 Place the larger wreath over the stand. Loop the ribbon onto the hooks at the top and secure.

4 Repeat step 2 with the smaller wreath and four pieces of ribbon, each $18\frac{1}{2}$ inches long. Place the small wreath over the stand so it hangs just above the larger wreath. Thread a piece of florist's wire through the ribbon loops and attach them to the hooks on the stand.

5 Using the wider ribbon, make four bows. Attach them to the ribbon loops around the smaller wicker wreath.

6 Decorate the wreaths with floral sprays and the remaining ribbon.

TABLE RUNNER

MATERIALS

(for one lengthwise and one widthwise runner)

$2\frac{1}{4}$ yards fabric
Scissors
Tape measure
Pins
4 tassels
$11\frac{1}{2}$ yards cord
Needle and thread

1 For the lengthwise runner, cut two pieces of fabric, each measuring 78 x $13\frac{1}{2}$ inches. Fold in half along the length and measure 8 inches from both corners of the folded edge across to the outside edge to form the angle of the point at each end (see diagram). Cut along this line at both ends.

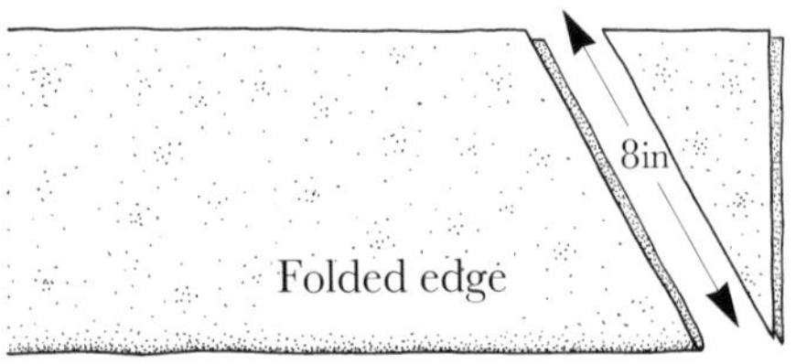

2 Unfold the fabric and pin a tassel to each of the longest points on the right side of one piece of fabric. Pin it with the fringed edge facing away from the cut edge. Baste the cord around the edge of the right side of the same runner piece, $\frac{1}{4}$ inch from the edge, over the end of the tassel.

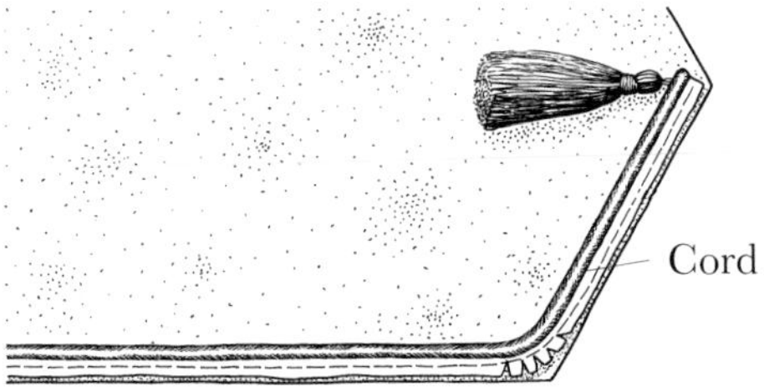

3 Place the two pieces of the table runner together, with right sides facing, and stitch around the outside edge next to the cord, leaving a $\frac{1}{4}$ inch seam allowance. Leave an 8 inch

opening for turning. Clip the corners and turn the runner the right way out. Hand-stitch the opening closed. Press.

4 To make the widthwise runner, cut two pieces of fabric, each measuring 52 x 13½ inches. Repeat steps 1 to 3.

NAPKIN RINGS

MATERIALS

(for one napkin ring)

Small wicker wreath, 2 inches in diameter
Gold spray-paint
Scissors
Cardboard tube (from a roll of paper towels)
Glue
14 inches gold-edged wine-colored moiré ribbon, 1½ inches wide
19 inches cream or ivory gathered lace, ½ inch wide
8 inches fused pearl strand
7 ribbon rosebuds

1 Spray the wicker wreath with gold paint in a well-ventilated area. Let dry.

2 Cut a 1½-inch wide section from the cardboard tube. Glue ribbon over the outside of the cardboard tube. Glue lace around both inside edges of the tube. Glue ribbon around the inside of the tube, covering the edge of glued lace.

3 Wrap the pearl strand around the wreath, and secure with glue. Glue the remaining lace around the outside edge of the wicker wreath.

4 Glue the wreath to the ribbon-covered cardboard tube. Decorate with ribbon rosebuds, gluing them down to secure.

Table runner and napkin rings

Room Decorations

The Victorians spent a great deal of time preparing their homes for the Christmas celebrations. They lavishly adorned every conceivable corner with garlands, bows, and sprays of ivy, holly, or evergreen. Fragrant foliage was draped over picture frames, along bannisters and balustrades, and around fireplace mantelpieces. Wreaths could be found hung on doors or behind windowpanes. The Victorian stores did not have a wide selection of readymade seasonal items to purchase, as we have today. Therefore, many natural elements found in the meadows and woodlands were used against a backdrop of fresh, rich greenery; flowers, pinecones, berries, and fruit were all used to create colorful displays.

You, too, can add a touch of Victorian charm to your Christmas decorations by making your own swags to hang over fireplaces, picture frames, or bannisters. Invite other members of the family to get involved and share the fun of creative crafting, as enjoyed by the Victorians.

VICTORIAN SWAG

Artificial garlands are easily available in most Christmas decoration departments. They can be decorated in many creative ways to complement other ornaments in the room setting. By making your own swag, whether it is from fresh, dried, or preserved greenery, you can add greater variety of color, texture, and fullness to the garland.

If you want a garland that can be used year after year, use artificial greenery for the base and tuck in a few fresh branches here and there. Dried or preserved greenery gives the more realistic look of a fresh garland, and has the advantage that it can be used on more than one occasion.

Making swags from fresh foliage is both quick and easy. Handmade garlands have a much fuller shape and add a dramatic backdrop for other decorations. They provide a fragrance that sets the seasonal ambience.

MATERIALS

Rope or thick cord
Fresh, dried, or preserved greenery
Pruning shears
20–22 gauge florist's or craft wire

1 Form a small loop at one end of the rope and tie a knot. Form a loop at the other end, once you have determined the desired length of the swag, taking into account any draping.

2 Cut the greenery into small sprigs. Wire up bunches of greenery with three small sprigs per bunch. Wire three bunches of greenery to one end of the rope. Wrap the wire around the already-wired end of the bunch, with the loose tips overlapping the loop. Wire one bunch at the back, and the remaining two in front.

3 Wire a second grouping of three bunches around the rope, moving a little farther along the rope so the greenery covers the wire from the previous foliage. Continue adding bunches of wired foliage until you reach the end of the rope.

4 Turn some greenery bunches to lie in the opposite direction, and wire them between the bunches already in place.

5 Position the swag in place and decorate.

CHAPTER 7

A Country Theme

IN TODAY'S MODERN WORLD, commercialism threatens to overcome every aspect of our lives. For this country theme, I have looked to nature for a less artificial approach to the decoration of tree and home.

By observing the profusion of natural materials that can be found in the woods and fields, along the highways and riverbanks, you can create your own country-style decorations to imitate the glorious wealth of beauty found in nature. The materials for this theme can be collected throughout the year, with each season providing its own contribution.

The same choice of nature's goodies are used throughout the home, from the welcoming wreath, the Christmas tree, and swag, to the festive table. Why not use a family excursion to give each member the opportunity of contributing to the seasonal decorations? With little expense and lots of creative satisfaction, you can build on your country theme from one year to the next.

Tree Decorations

On the country Christmas tree, I have used bows made from burlap ribbon to hold up the cocoa rope swag. The tree is lit by the use of tiny white tree lights, so the honeycomb candles in rope-covered pots are for decoration only. Small rose-filled terracotta pots and nut baskets peek out from the collection of cinnamon-stick bundles, preserved oranges, pinecones, colorful fabric hearts, and gilded cookies. The whole array is guarded by a burlap treetop angel and her band of heavenly colleagues.

HANGING CANDLES

MATERIALS

Scissors
40 inches dark, natural-fiber rope, such as cocoa rope (for each hanging candle)
Low-temperature glue gun and glue sticks
Terracotta flowerpots, 1½ inches high and 1¾ inches in diameter
Honeycomb candles, 4 inches high and ¾ inch in diameter
Flat moss

1 Cut a 10½-inch piece of cocoa rope and form it into a loop so the ends lie side by side (not end to end). Glue the ends of the rope loop to the inside of a terracotta flowerpot.

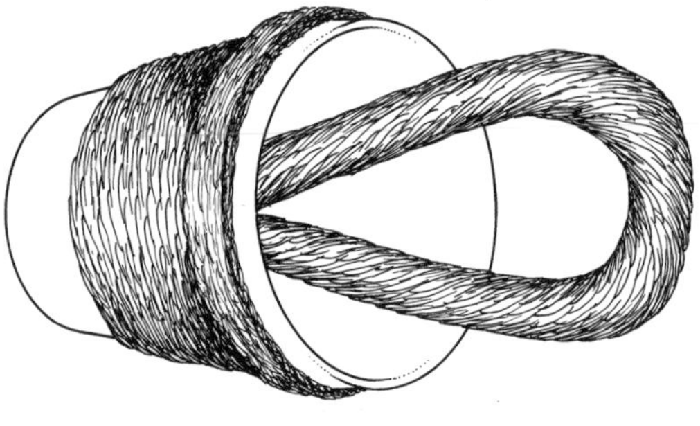

2 Coil the remaining rope around the outside of the terracotta pot, gluing it in place.

3 Glue the candle in the center of the pot and stuff flat moss around it to hold it in place. Repeat to make as many hanging candles as you like.

CAUTION: These candles are for decoration only. Lit candles can be a serious fire hazard on a tree.

TERRACOTTA POTS WITH ROSES

MATERIALS

90-gauge wire
Terracotta flowerpots, 1½ inches high and 1¾ inches in diameter
Dry florist's foam
Flat moss
Dried rosebuds (3 per pot)

1 Bend a 12-inch piece of wire in half. Thread one half of the wire up through the hole at the bottom of a terracotta flowerpot to the lip at the top of the pot. The other half of the wire should remain on the outside of the terracotta pot.

Hanging candle, terracotta pot with roses, and preserved orange slices (page 112)

2 Twist the two ends of the folded wire together as neatly as possible. This wire can then be used to attach the completed pot to the tree.

3 Pack the inside of the terracotta pot with dry florist's foam and cover the top of the foam with flat moss.

4 Poke a 6-inch piece of wire through the bottom of a rosebud, about 3/8 inch from the stem. Twist the ends of the wire together. Poke three wired rosebuds into each pot.

PRESERVED ORANGE SLICES

Materials

Fruit knife
Fresh, firm oranges
Paper towels
Low-temperature glue gun and glue sticks
Raffia

1 Slice the oranges about 1/4 inch thick. Put two layers of paper towels in a microwaveable dish. Place the slices of two oranges, one at a time, on top of the paper towels.

2 Bake the orange slices in a microwave oven on high for about 6 to 10 minutes, until the slices turn very bright yellow. The length of time will vary, depending on how juicy the oranges are and the strength of the oven. When you remove the orange slices, they will be sticky and spongy to the touch, and the paper towels will be saturated. You may need to experiment with this stage.

3 Place the orange slices in a preheated oven on the lowest possible temperature, and bake for about 45 minutes. Watch the oranges carefully and test them often. The time can vary according to the texture of the orange, the type of oven, and the air humidity.

4 To assemble the ornaments, take three slices and cut two of them in half. Glue the four halves on each side of the remaining whole slice at a 45° angle (see the diagram).

Country angel and country hearts (page 114)

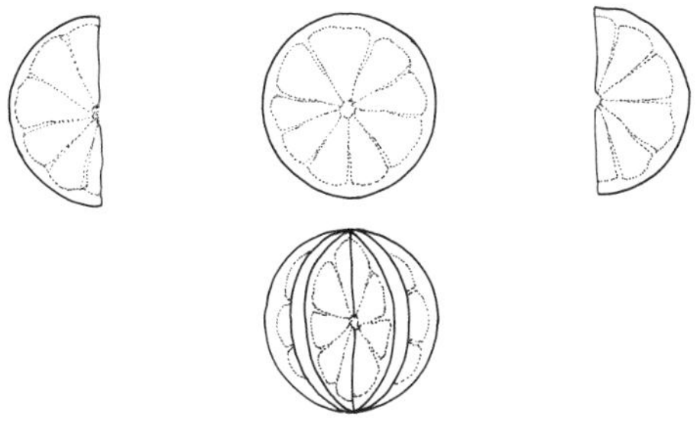

5 Poke a hole in the top of one end of the whole orange slice, thread through a piece of raffia, and knot it to form a hanging loop.

COUNTRY ANGEL

MATERIALS

These amounts below are for making the treetop angel. You can make smaller angel tree ornaments by reducing the materials proportionately.

1 wooden head bead, 1¾ inch long
Acrylic paints
Small paintbrush
Cotton swab
Cosmetic powder blusher
Fusible web
Burlap, 12 inches square
Lightweight, flexible board
Tracing paper
Pencil
Scissors
Ruler
Low-temperature glue gun and glue sticks
Clothespin
Spanish moss
28-gauge gold-colored wire
Raffia
Small beads
18 inches burlap ribbon

1 Paint the wooden head bead with flesh-colored acrylic paint. When dry, paint black eyes using the rounded end of the brush handle. Add a twinkle to the angel's eyes by painting a tiny dot in the outer corner of each eye. Dab a cotton swab in cosmetic powder blusher, then dab it on the bead to create cheeks.

2 Following the manufacturer's directions, fuse the burlap to one side of the board using fusible web. Trace the pattern (see page 123) on the board side and cut out. Cut out two 3-inch squares of burlap.

3 To make the dress/body, form the scalloped piece into a cone shape by lining up the last scallop on each end. Glue the edges together and hold with a clothespin until dry.

4 Form the sleeves/arms by rolling each 3-inch square of burlap into a cone shape by overlapping and gluing the opposite corners. Rolling the board around a pencil first makes the sleeves easier to form.

5 Glue the sleeves to the sides of the larger cone by lining them up; the small point of the arms should be at the top, and the seam should be along the edge to be glued.

6 Glue the wooden head bead over the point of the large cone. Glue moss to the back of the head bead to form hair. Make a circular halo with 4 inches of wire, leaving ½ inch free at each end. Twist the ends together and bend at right angles to the circle. Glue this inside the back of the hair.

7 Tie a small raffia bow and glue this under the head bead (chin) at the front. Glue a few small beads down from the bow to create the illusion of buttons.

8 Fold the cut ends of the burlap ribbon to the center, overlapping them slightly. Wrap wire around the center to form a large bow. Glue this to the angel's back for the wings.

COUNTRY HEARTS

MATERIALS

Pinking shears or straight-edged scissors
Scraps of cotton fabric (small Christmas print)
Batting
Needle and thread
Raffia
Fabric glue

1 Using the pattern given on page 122, cut out at least two hearts from the same cotton fabric. Use pinking shears for a serrated edge, or straight-edged scissors for a frayed edge. Cut out a piece of batting $^1/_4$ inch smaller than the pattern.

2 With wrong sides together, hand-stitch the two fabric hearts together, $^1/_4$ inch from the cut edge, leaving a small opening.

3 Insert the piece of batting through the opening, and stitch the opening to close.

4 Make a loop with a length of raffia. Glue to the front of the heart where it dips at the top. Tie a small raffia bow and glue it over the cut ends of the raffia loop. Repeat the steps to make more country hearts.

MINIATURE BASKET OF NUTS

MATERIALS

Scissors
Cocoa rope
Low-temperature glue gun and glue sticks
Small rectangular basket
Dry florist's foam
Flat moss
Mixture of nuts and small pinecones

1 Cut a 4-inch piece of cocoa rope. Glue each end to the opposite sides of the inside of the basket.

2 Stuff the basket with florist's foam. Cover the outside edges of the basket and a little of the florist's foam with flat moss.

3 Glue nuts and small pinecones over the florist's foam, building up layers that spill out over the sides of the basket, as shown opposite.

CHRISTMAS COOKIES

MATERIALS

Mixing bowl
Wooden spoon
$^1/_2$ cup softened butter
$1^1/_4$ cup confectioner's sugar
1 egg yolk
2 teaspoons vanilla extract
Sifter
2 cups all-purpose flour
Rolling pin
Baking parchment or waxed paper
Cookie cutters
Skewer or toothpick
Gold spray-paint
Raffia

1 Preheat the oven to 325°F. In a mixing bowl, beat together the butter, sugar, egg yolk, and vanilla extract, until the mixture is creamy and light. Gradually sift in the flour and mix to a soft dough.

2 Roll out the dough between sheets of baking parchment or waxed paper, until it is about $^1/_4$ inch thick. Cut the dough into varying shapes using cookie cutters.

Christmas cookies, miniature baskets of nuts, and preserved orange slices (see page 112)

3 Using a skewer or toothpick, poke a hole in each cookie. It should be large enough to thread raffia through.

4 Bake the cookies for 20 minutes on the top shelf of the oven. Remove and leave to cool.

CAUTION: These cookies are for decoration only and should not be eaten, so hang them out of reach of very young children.

5 In a well-ventilated area, spray both the front and back of the cookies with a light coat of gold spray-paint. Allow to dry.

6 When the cookies are completely dry, thread a 10-inch piece of raffia through each, and tie the ends together to form a hanging loop.

Room Decorations

Extend the festive country theme throughout your home by making one of the projects in this section. The elaborate country Christmas swag, made using an attractive selection of dried and preserved seed heads, cones, and fruit, would look wonderful draped above a mantelpiece. Alternatively, you can make a resplendent wreath for the front door using an abundance of natural ingredients, including oranges, lemons, cinnamon, and chili peppers. When you look at nature's harvest, you will find a wealth of materals you can plunder for use in room decorations.

COUNTRY CHRISTMAS SWAG

MATERIALS

7 feet wire-edged ribbon
90-gauge florist's wire
Low-temperature glue gun and glue sticks
Dried rosebuds or nuts
Homemade evergreen swag (see pages 106-107)
Dried artichokes
Gold spray-paint
Cinnamon sticks
Raffia
Artificial pomegranates
Poppy heads
Freeze-dried whole oranges
Preserved orange slices (see page 112)
Assorted cones
Chili peppers
Country hearts made from burlap (see page 114)

1 Form two large bows using 44 inches of wire-edged ribbon for each bow. Do not tie the bows, but secure them in place by wrapping wire around the centers. Glue a cluster of nuts to the center of each, covering the wire. Wire one bow into each corner of the homemade evergreen swag.

2 In a well-ventilated area, lightly gild the dried artichokes with gold spray-paint. When dry, twist wire around the stem of each artichoke, and attach the artichokes to the swag.

3 Make up the cinnamon-stick bunches by tying three or four sticks together with raffia. Wrap a 10-inch piece of wire around the raffia at the back of the bundle. Twist the ends together and use the raffia to attach the bunch to the swag.

4 Poke a hole in one end of each pomegranate. Taking each pomegranate in turn, glue one end of a piece of wire in the hole. To attach the pomegranate to the swag, twist the wire end into the swag.

5 Using wire, tie about seven poppy heads into a bunch. Cover the wire with raffia. Use the wire to attach the bunch to the swag.

6 Poke a piece of wire through one end of the freeze-dried whole oranges and orange

Opposite *Country Christmas swag*

slices in turn. Wire them together in groups, then attach them to the swag with wire.

7 Fill in the gaps and spaces on the swag by wiring on groups of assorted cones and chili peppers (in bunches of five), together with the country hearts.

COUNTRY CHRISTMAS DOOR WREATH

Materials

Low-temperature glue gun and glue sticks
90-gauge wire, cut into 12-inch lengths
Twigs
Moss-covered wreath, 16 inches in diameter
Raffia
6 freeze-dried oranges
12 Preserved Orange Slices (see page 112)
24 poppy heads
4 artificial pomegranates
6 lotus heads (or any distinctive dried-flower head)
20 cinnamon sticks
Assorted pods, as available (I used rose de tefé and brachychiton)
Assorted cones
Dried chili peppers

1 Glue or wire small twigs to the back of the moss-covered wreath so they protrude around the outside edge of the wreath.

2 Take a handful of long raffia strands and tie the strands into an 8-inch bow (when measured across the width of the loops). Glue the bow to the top of the wreath.

3 Using the glue gun, attach four groups of whole preserved oranges and orange slices to the wreath. I have made two groups of one freeze-dried orange and three preserved slices; the remaining two groups each have two whole oranges and three preserved slices.

4 Prepare three bunches of eight poppy heads by wiring them together. Position and wire them to the wreath.

5 Poke a hole in one end of each pomegranate and glue in one end of wire. Twist two pomegranate wires together, and wire to the wreath.

6 Poke a wire through the bottom end of the lotus heads. Bring the wire ends together and twist. Make two groups of lotus heads by wiring three heads together for each group. Wire the groups to the wreath.

7 Make five cinnamon-stick bundles by tying four or more sticks together with raffia. Glue the bundles to the wreath.

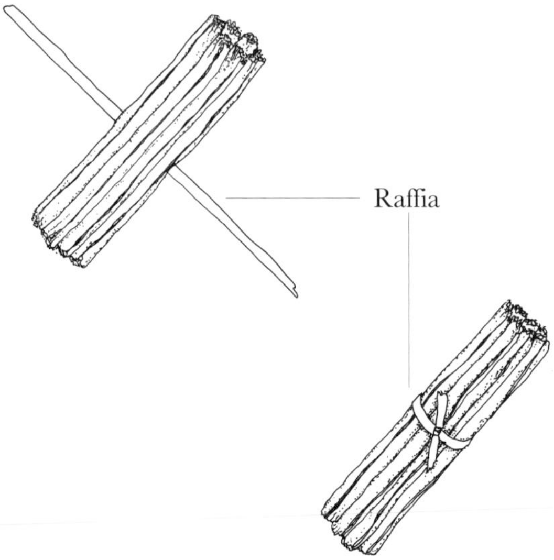

8 Fill in the remaining gaps on the wreath by gluing on various assorted pods, cones, and bunches of chili peppers.

Opposite *Country Christmas door wreath*

Table Setting

Study the lush abundance of fruit, rich with nature's autumnal bounty, overflowing from the candle display of our table centerpiece. It joins the mulled wine and homemade mince pies in anticipation of the feast ahead, while napkin rings are quickly put together using cinnamon-stick bundles decorated with preserved orange slices, dried rosebuds, and little cones.

TABLE CENTERPIECE

MATERIALS

Three-candle basket
Dry florist's foam
Green flat moss
90-gauge wire
Green preserved beech
Rustic-colored preserved tree ivy with berries
Assorted cones of various sizes
3–5 lotus heads (or any distinctive dried-flower head)
16 poppy heads
6 protea buds (or any distinctive dried-flower bud)
Preserved Orange Slices
(see page 112)
Low-temperature glue gun and glue sticks
3 freeze-dried whole oranges
3 freeze-dried whole lemons
3 artificial apples
6 artificial plums
3 artificial pomegranates
3 pods
Dried chili peppers
Cinnamon sticks
Raffia
3 cream-colored candles, 12 inches long and 1 inch in diameter

1 Fill the center of the candle basket with florist's foam and cover with green flat moss.

2 Wire together six bunches of green beech, and insert them into the florist's foam. Spread them evenly over the center of the basket.

3 Wire together three bunches of tree ivy with berries. Insert them into the florist's foam, spreading them evenly between the beech bunches.

4 Wire together six groups of various sizes and types of cone. To wire a cone, take a 10-inch piece of wire and wrap it around the bottom (wider) edge of the cone through the scales. Bring the two wires together and twist.

5 Poke a 10-inch wire through the bottom end of the lotus heads. Bring the wire ends together and twist. Spread three to five of the wired lotus heads evenly throughout the arrangement.

6 Wire poppy heads into four groups of between three and five heads, and insert them into the florist's foam around the arrangement. Position six protea buds individually around the arrangement.

7 Wire together three groups of preserved orange slices and insert them into the arrangement. Glue three freeze-dried whole oranges and three freeze-dried whole lemons into the arrangement.

8 Add three artifical apples and three groups of two artificial plums, which have been wired together. Poke three wired artificial pomegranates into the arrangement.

CAUTION: Burning candles should never be left unattended.

Table centerpiece

9 Fill in any gaps with the pods and the chili peppers. Finish off the center of the arrangement with small bunches of cinnamon sticks tied together with raffia. Place the candles into the basket rings, and pack with moss.

Templates

ALL TEMPLATES are actual size, unless otherwise stated. When tracing half-templates, flip the tracing paper to trace the mirror image for the other half.

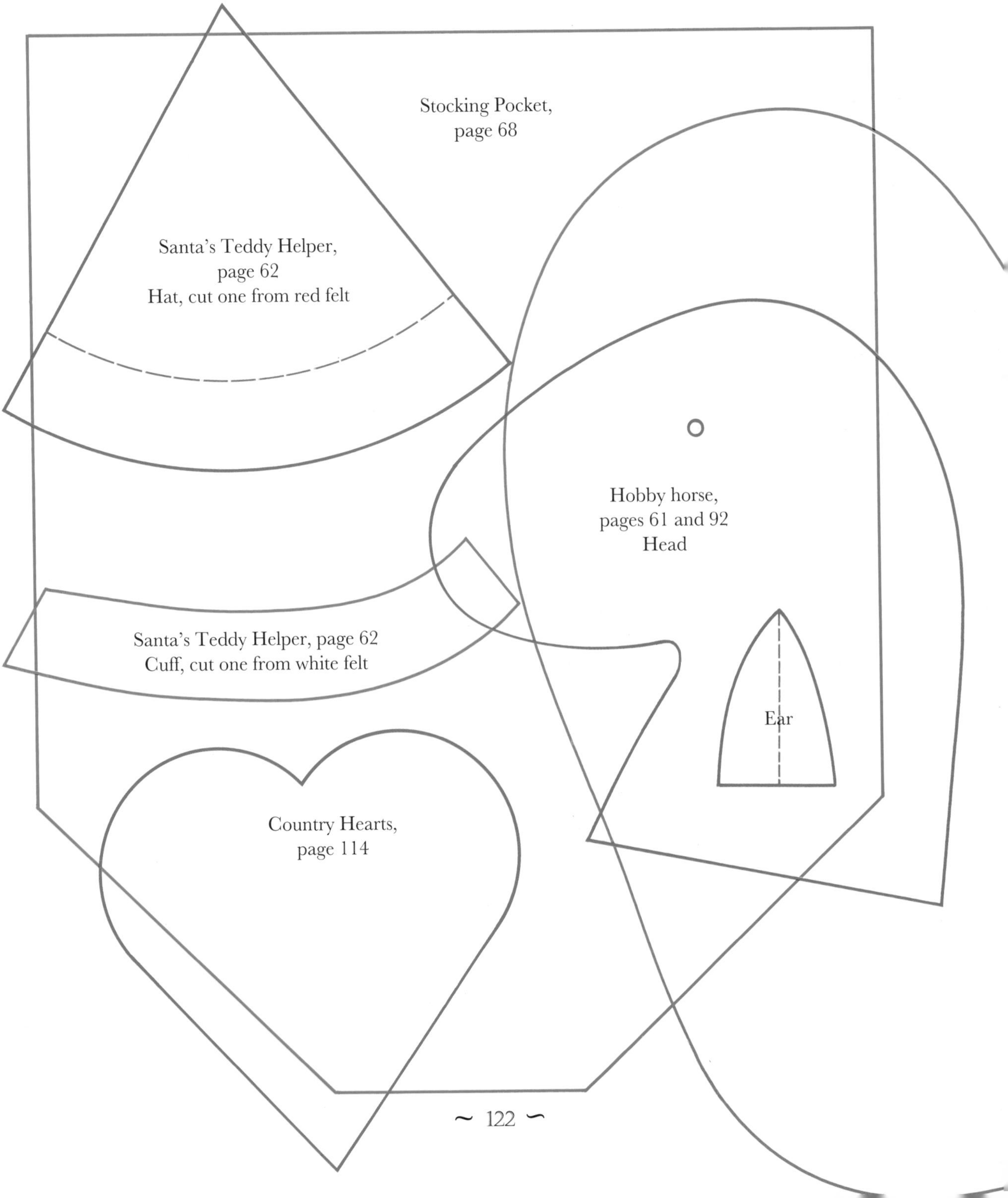

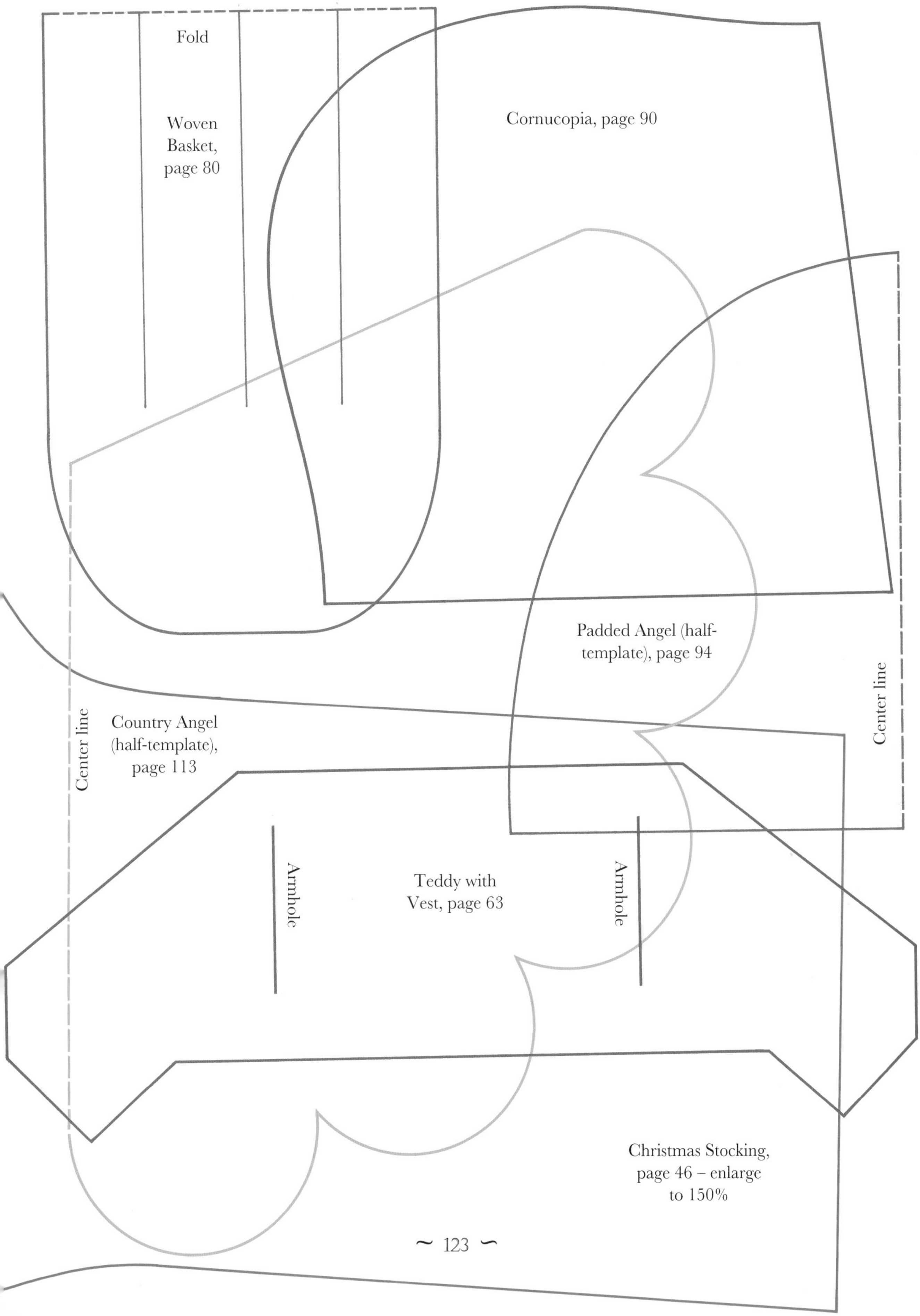
Fold
Woven Basket, page 80
Cornucopia, page 90
Padded Angel (half-template), page 94
Center line
Center line
Country Angel (half-template), page 113
Armhole
Teddy with Vest, page 63
Armhole
Christmas Stocking, page 46 – enlarge to 150%

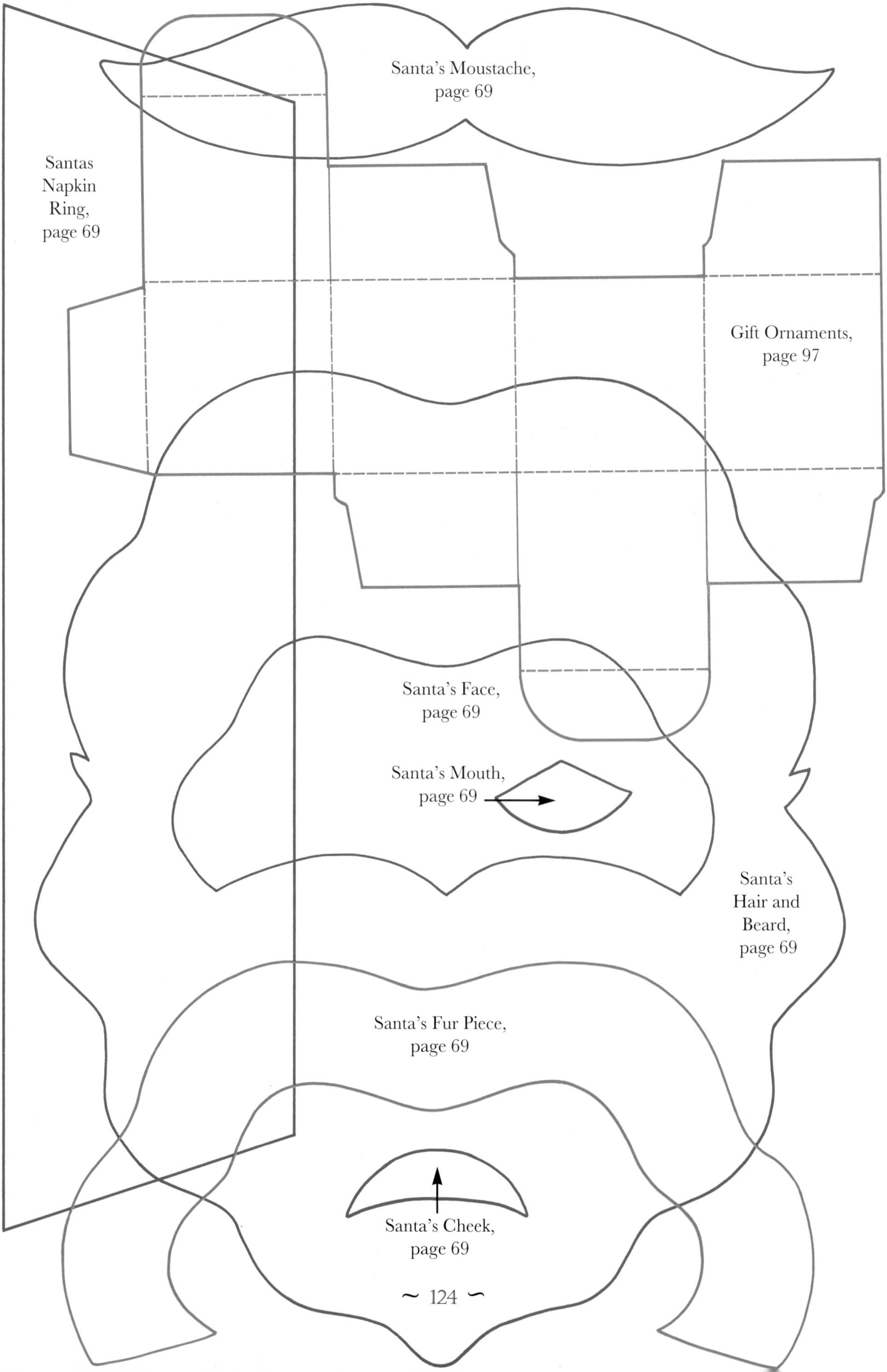
Santa's Moustache, page 69
Santas Napkin Ring, page 69
Gift Ornaments, page 97
Santa's Face, page 69
Santa's Mouth, page 69
Santa's Hair and Beard, page 69
Santa's Fur Piece, page 69
Santa's Cheek, page 69

Beaded Table Linen,
page 32

Acknowledgments

I would like to say a very special thank you to the following for all their help in completing this book:

Debbie Vertrees for designing and making decorations. Debbie not only made up the projects from designs I had in mind, but she also contributed ideas and designs of her own, particularly in the tartan, toyland, and Victorian chapters.

Marion Wright for making decorations, and designing and dressing trees. Marion was my faithful assistant without whom this book would have taken another four years! She made samples and designs to specification, and spent early mornings and late nights completing the decorations and helping to decorate the trees, swags, and tables.

Laila Paulsen-Becjac and **Kari Paulsen** for making projects and advising on the Scandinavian chapter. Kari gave me the idea of including a Scandinavian theme with her wonderful stories of Christmas in Norway and the fascinating decorations she had in her home every Christmas. Laila helped to source materials and collected information. She also as translated, made up many of the various projects, and designed the little *Julenisser*.

Bitte Kendal for advising on the Scandinavian chapter. Bitte spent hours telling me all about her early memories of the Christmas festivities from her childhood in Denmark, giving me ideas and background for the Scandinavian chapter.

Nancy Godsmark for making stiffened bows. Nancy is the best bow-maker I know. She is responsible for making the projects with the gorgeous "Stiffy" bows in the tartan chapter.

Liz Davies and **Diane Mutkin** for designing and preparing projects in the country chapter. Liz and Diane have a very special and unique talent, which corresponded with my idea of a country Christmas theme.

Janet Cooper, Anne Flynn, Carol Nelson, and Kathy Sanders for making decorations for the tree.

Tina Guillory for finding the most wonderful photography locations. She was a most helpful and encouraging stylist during the hectic and difficult photography sessions.

Caroline Arber took the most wonderful photographs. Her attention to detail and artistic talent has made the photography in this book superb.

Heather Dewhurst, who so patiently edited my many words and diagrams to make them into something quite wonderful!

I would like to thank the following companies for allowing us to use their products:

The Beadery supplied beads and gemstones, and allowed us to use their "Icicles" and "Winter Wonderland" designs (available in kit form) in the Victorian chapter.

Creative Beadcraft Ltd. provided the beads, pearls, sequins, filigree findings, and braids for the pincraft ornaments and other decorations throughout the book.

Newey Goodman Ltd. supplied the pins for the pincraft ornaments.

CM Offray & Son Ltd. supplied all the ribbons used throughout the book.

Panduro Hobby kindly provided the materials for the Scandinavian chapter.

Plaid Enterprises for use of "Folkart" acrylic and spray-paints; "Mod Podge" water-based glaze; "Stiffy" fabric stiffener; "Paper Capers" paper ribbon; "Fashion Fabric Paint"; "Shaper Paper" wire-edged paper ribbon.

Porth Innovations Ltd. provided the artificial trees used in the step-by-step and colour theme chapters (sometimes at very short notice).

Rita Snelling at **Rainbow Ribbons** supplied the candy dish for the color themes table setting.

Therm0Web for providing the fusible web.

The rocking horse in our Toyland Christmas Tree photograph is a medium-sized FH Ayres horse on a safety stand. It is a faithful reproduction of a Victorian horse, and is hand-stippled, and with horsehair mane and tail, and leather tack. Lent by Stevenson Bros, The Workshops, Ashford Road, Bethersden, Kent N26 3PA (Tel: 01233 820363).

All tree lights were kindly provided by Noma Lites and are available from good department stores and garden centers.

All glassware, cutlery, and china were very kindly lent by Aldis Superstores of Fakenham, Norwich (Tel: 01328-855327), who also supplied carpets, furniture, and linen.

The tree in the Victorian chapter was lent by Fakenham Garden Center of Norfolk.

The bears in the toyland chapter photographs were lent by The Bear Shop at both 18 Elm Hill, Norwich (Tel: 01603 766866) and 3 Sir Isaacs Walk, Colchester, Essex (Tel: 01206 577345).

Index

Page numbers in *italics* refer to illustrations